REICH RAILS

ABOUT THE AUTHOR

Blaine Taylor (*b*. 1946) is the American author of twenty illustrated histories on war, politics, automotives, biography, engineering, architecture, medicine, photography, and aviation.

The well-read historian is a former Vietnam War soldier and Military Policeman of the U.S. Army's elite 199th Light Infantry Brigade under enemy Communist Viet Cong fire during 1966–67 in the now defunct South Vietnam. He was awarded twelve medals and decorations, including the coveted Combat Infantryman's Badge/CIB. A later crime and political newspaper reporter, Mr Taylor also is an award-winning medical journalist, international magazine writer, and the winner of four political campaigns as press secretary for county, state, and U.S. Presidential elections.

During 1991–92, he served as a U.S. Congressional aide and press secretary on Capitol Hill, Washington, DC.

His previously published book titles are:

Guarding the Fuhrer: Sepp Dietrich, Johann Rattenhuber, and the Protection of Adolf Hitler (1993)

Fascist Eagle: Italy's Air Marshal Italo Balbo (1996)

Mercedes-Benz Parade and Staff Cars of the Third Reich (1999)

Volkswagen Military Vehicles of the Third Reich (2004)

Hitler's Headquarters from Beer Hall to Bunker1920–45 (2006)

Hitlerovy Hlavni Stany: Z Pivnice do Dunkru, 1920–45 (Slovak language edition of the above title 2007)

Apex of Glory: Benz, Daimler, & Mercedes-Benz 1885–1955 (2006)

Hitler's Chariots Volume I: Mercedes-Benz G-4 Cross-Country Touring Car (2009)

Hitler's Chariots Volume 2: Mercedes-Benz 770K Grosser Parade Car (2010)

Hitler's Engineers: Fritz Todt and Albert Speer/Master Builders of the Third Reich (2010)

Inzynierowie tajna armia Hitlera (Polish language edition of the above title, (2011)

Hitler's Chariots Volume 3: Volkswagen from Nazi People's Car to New Beetle (2011)

Mrs Adolf Hitler: The Eva Braun Photograph Albums (2013)

Dallas Fifty Years On: The Murder of John F. Kennedy (2013)

Guarding the Fuhrer: Sepp Dietrich & Adolf Hitler/Upgraded Edition (2014)

Hermann Goering in the First World War: The Personal Photograph Albums of Hermann Goering (2014)

Kaiser Bill! A New Look at Germany's Last Emperor Wilhelm II 1859–1941 (2014)

Hitlerovi Inzenyri: Fritz Todt a Albert Speer/Hlavni stavitele Treti rise (Slovak language edition of *Hitler's Engineer's* 2015)

Hermann Goering: Beer Hall Putsch to Nazi Blood Purge 1919–34 (2015)

REICH RAILS

ROYAL PRUSSIA, IMPERIAL GERMANY
AND THE FIRST WORLD WAR
1835–1918

BLAINE TAYLOR

FONTHILL

Fonthill Media Language Policy

Fonthill Media publishes in the international English language market. One language edition is published worldwide. As there are minor differences in spelling and presentation, especially with regard to American English and British English, a policy is necessary to define which form of English to use. The Fonthill Policy is to use the form of English native to the author. Blaine Taylor was born at Washington, D.C., educated at Towson University, and now lives at Towson, MD, therefore American English has been adopted in this publication.

Fonthill Media Limited
Fonthill Media LLC
www.fonthillmedia.com
office@fonthillmedia.com

First published in the United Kingdom
and the United States of America 2016

British Library Cataloguing in Publication Data:
A catalogue record for this book is available from the British Library

Copyright © Blaine Taylor 2016

ISBN 978-1-78155-424-1

Typeset in 10.5pt on 13pt Sabon
Printed and bound by CPI Group (UK) Ltd, Croydon, CR0 4YY

To former Maryland State House of Delegates twice elected Member Jacob Mohorovic Jr. (D, 7th)—1971 Taylor Towson State College Student Government Association Presidential campaign manager, and his wife, Janice Horak Mohorovic—both Class of 1974, now Towson University, MD, for their many decades of treasured friendship and always wise counsel.

DEARLY DEPARTED

Juan Alzamora (1968–2016), who died March 2016. He and his family came to the U.S. legally from Peru, and I met him when he was 19 with a sister, I was 45, and we were all out dancing. He was then working as a busboy, put himself through computer school with an earned degree, went to work for the U.S. Army as a civilian, married, and had two wonderful children. I was a guest at their wedding. His death from cancer came totally unexpected to me, and was therefore a great shock. I loved him as a brother, and will always remember him. Go with God, my friend, RIP.

Richard Dale Neidig (1947–2016), who died 16 July 2016, former political opponent and elected Towson State College, MD Student Government Association President, 1970–71. RIP.

Preface

A Love Affair with Trains

On 8 August 1968, I saw and heard on American television then-Republican Party Presidential nominee Richard M. Nixon give his acceptance speech of his nomination at Miami Beach, Florida. In it, he recalled himself as a young boy growing up in California decades before thus: "He hears the train go by at night, and dreams of faraway places he would like to go. It seems an impossible dream."

To an extent, 10 years earlier—living in a three-story, walk-up tenement house in a run-down area of Baltimore called Waverly—I had another dream while watching passing trains at night from my bed, looking out the window. By the year 2003, I had long ago achieved my dream of becoming a published book author, but I still was riveted by the magical sounds of a train passing by in the night. This time, however, I found myself ensconced alone in the majestic, vast spaces of the Eisenhower Suite of the Thayer Hotel on the grounds of the United States Military Academy at West Point, NY. The suite alone was larger than my entire balcony apartment at Towson, MD, where I still live and write, and where this book was written. The train that I heard that night outside the sleepy town of Highland Falls, NY—that is immediately adjacent to the USMA—was and is the West Shore Railroad.

As its train rumbled past each night that I stayed there, I wondered if it woke up the USMA cadets in their dormitory halls not far from me—or had they long ago gotten used to it, as I had in Waverly, 45 years before? I expect that they had.

I have been fascinated by the lore of trains all my life. I have probably seen—time and again—almost every train movie ever made. I thoroughly enjoyed the times that I have taken the train from Baltimore to New York, watching the countryside fly by my window *en route*.

Train rides, I've found, help me put the fast pace of daily life into a more relaxed perspective, and perhaps that is one reason why I have enjoyed them so much. I mused alone to myself about the houses and homes I saw along the way, wondering who lived in them, what they did, and how their lives were going.

Like so much else in our modern lives, very soon after their invention by men, trains became instruments first of diplomacy, then of war, and—in the twentieth century—of the Holocaust to kill the Jews and others.

Without rails and the engines and cars that rode on them, modern wars since 1859 would not have been fought and won or lost, at least not in the way that they were. Indeed, without them, the Holocaust simply would not have been possible, or executed as it was. As with my previous car books, this, too, is a study of the machinery of transportation, but it is also—as with those earlier volumes as well—of many small biographies of the men and women who rode them.

The trains used were not robots, and thus they required human masters to run them.

Herein, I trace the martial history of trains from their invention through the wars in which their usage was perfected, and up through the end of the First World War, 1914–18.

Blaine Taylor
Berkshires at Town Center
Towson, MD
Centennial of the Great War, 1914–18

1 August 2016

Contents

Acknowledgments

Thanks to Herr Alfred Gottwaldt, Senior Curator, German Technical Museum, Berlin, author; the German Railway Society, to Mrs. Erika Burke, translator, Pearland, TX; Photographic Consultant Stan Piet, Bel Air, MD, and to Publisher Alan Sutton, who is making it possible. All helped in the production of this work, and I am grateful to all of them.

1

Railroads in Peace and War, 1828–71

Genesis

The invention of the all-important steam engine occurred during the Industrial Revolution in England, first by Thomas Newcomen, and then by James Watt in 1769. That same year, Frenchman Nicholas Cugnot's first steam powered vehicle proved to be impractical. In 1804, the first steam engine pulled cars known as wagons within a dirty Welsh ironworks during the English Industrial Revolution.

At the outset of the Nineteenth Century, Englishman George Stephenson built the world's first truly functional steam locomotive, and in 1825, there appeared the globe's first railway as well. It employed the Stephenson steam engine on the route from Stockton to Darlington in the United Kingdom. The first modern French steam railway appeared in 1837, running from Paris to Le Pecq.

Modern railroads began in 1676 at England's Newcastle on wooden planks and rails, over which rode small coal cars pulled by animals. By placing iron sheets over the wooden rails underneath, wear and tear was thereby reduced. Thus, late in the Eighteenth Century, the wooden rails themselves were made of iron instead.

Cast in an L-shape, the iron rail's upright part stood two-three inches high, the L-shape being added on one side of each to keep the wheels safely on the track underneath.

In 1789—the year that the French Revolution broke out on the Continent—the Butterlee Ironworks' William Jessup introduced the concept of placing the projected part not on the iron rails, but rather on the wheels instead, thus having them glide over the upright part of the L, with the flanged wheel projecting downward, along the sides. Over time, it was these edged rails that evolved into today's universally used rail types that we now know.

The initial railways were their owners' private transportation exclusively, but 1825's Stockton & Darlington Railway debuted as the world's first for both freight *and* general population passenger service as well. British inventor Stephenson's steam locomotive became the prime vehicle for produced motive power, but in 1830, the Liverpool & Manchester Railway established the more modern steam-powered engine as the new industry's superior form.

Railway development in the United States started at about the same time as in the UK. The Baltimore & Ohio Railroad began in 1831. The years in which other countries first opened steam railways were: Austria and France, 1828; Belgium and Germany, 1835; Russia, 1838; Italy, 1839; Switzerland, 1844; Spain, 1848; Canada and Mexico, 1850; Sweden, 1851; Norway and India, 1853; Portugal, Brazil, and Australia, 1854; Egypt, 1856; South Africa and Turkey, 1860; Japan, 1872. In 1937, there were 788,672 miles of railways in the world, of which 233,670 miles—or about one third—were in the United States.

Long transcontinental lines have had an incalculable effect—politically and commercially—in consolidating the countries through which they run, opening vast areas to settlement and trade, and quickening transit from sea to sea. The first transcontinental route in North America was completed in 1869 by the junction of the Union Pacific and the Central Pacific between Omaha and San Francisco, and before the end of the Nineteenth Century, four others had been added.

In Canada, the Canadian Pacific (1885) was the first transcontinental line, stretching under one ownership from the Atlantic to the Pacific. In South America, the last section of a railway from Buenos Aires to the Chilean coast was finished in 1910. The Trans-Siberian Railway—giving through communication from European Russia across Asia to the Pacific—was completed in 1902, except for a short section at Lake Baikal, which was constructed in 1904, by the Russian tsar.

Early German Civilian Trains and Lines

According to the German Railway Society, the railway history of what is now Germany is complicated by the fact that it was the last major European country to be unified—the accomplishment of Otto von Bismarck—that took its final shape in 1871.

During the start-up growth years of railroading, Germany's multiple independent states *each* and *all* had their own concept of operation, including design. Indeed, some of these "Royal" railroads continued to exist into the 1920s, more than five decades after German national unification of all the individual states into one sovereign state as the German Reich/Empire had been achieved in 1871. It was not until 1 April 1920—following the loss of the Great War by Imperial Germany—that all the various German state Railways were finally forged as well in a single entity. It was known as the *Deutsche Reichsbahn Gessellschaft*, or by the acronym of *DRG*, using the simpler, iconic logo emblem of *DR*.

This new DRG immediately found itself as the manager of a vast array of not only differing locomotive engines, but also of rolling stock—passenger coaches and freight cars—as well.

Germany's own first locomotive railway engine had appeared in 1816. This initial engine failed, however, but was succeeded by another that worked in 1817. The country's truly modern railway history did not really start until 7 December 1835 as the later famous *Adler* [Eagle] began running along a five-mile line connecting Nuremberg and Fürth. Its own locomotive was English-built rather than German, by Stephenson & Company of Newcastle-on-Tyne, United Kingdom.

This British 2-2-2 Patented-type engine featured exterior frames plus a small diameter but high chimney, and soon achieved great popularity all over Europe and several other countries abroad, opening its first Netherlander line in 1839.

The *Adler* had both primitive frontal bumpers as well as others on it pulled tender, needed for both shunting work and reverse gear pulling. Thus, the *Adler* takes pride of place as Germany's first fully operational steam locomotive, with copies built in 1935 under the Third Reich. This initial *Adler* served until 1857, when its boiler was scrapped, its wheels and motion element being saved. Today, an *Adler* replica is displayed at the Nuremberg-Fürth Line Museum. The Prussian Berlin–Anhalt Railway debuted in 1843 led by a 2-2-2 engine with its own replica now shown at Munich's Science Museum. By 1845, there were 2,000 kilometers of operational German railways, and a decade later, more than 8,000 in a mixture of both private and Prussian state-owned lines. The *Eisenbahn* even included the first international railway that linked Cologne to Antwerp in 1846.

Bismarck's newly constituted German Empire of January 1871 consisted of 25 sovereign states, and some of these territories and kingdoms operated their own railroads, together called the *Landerbahnen* [Territorial Railways]: the Royal Railways of Prussia, Bavaria, Saxony, Württemburg, Baden, Mecklenburg, Oldenburg, Pfalz, Alsace-Lothringen, and the Ludwigsbahn.

In 1828, the King of Saxony founded the Dresden Technical School, where engineering Professor Johann Andreas Schubert designed a "German" steam locomotive based upon what he had seen in England,

Otto Eduard Leopold, Prince of
Bismarck, Duke of Lauenburg
(1815–1898), known as Otto von
Bismarck, photographed in 1862.

built by the Ubigauer Machine Building firm of Dresden from his plans. In 1838, Josef Anton Ritter von Maffei (1790–1870) manufactured in Munich the first Bavarian locomotive at the Eisenwerk/Iron Works at Hirschau. Two years later, the final section of the Munich-Augsburg railway line was designed by Paul Camille von Denis, who had earlier laid down the Nuremberg-Fürth line. That same year of 1838, the first Prussian railway line opened between Berlin and Potsdam, the suburban home of the Kings of Prussia. In 1842, the first saloon coach was built for the Grand Duchy of Baden.

The year 1850 saw the agreement of the principal dimensions of rolling stock by the various German railway firms, and in 1853, the first working rules were adopted for both Prussian and other North German railways. The following year witnessed the first steam railcar running on the Berlin–Hamburg line, and in 1857, the first international through coach was rolling on the line Frankfurt-am-Main to Basel in Switzerland.

In 1866, Krauss & Company was founded by Doctor of Engineering Georg von Krauss (1826–1906), with a Munich-based factory. In 1873, the first overnight sleeping car was built by the Nagelmaker firm. Unified signals were achieved for all of the new Reich in 1875, and three years later, the first Prussian standards for locomotives were promulgated for all locomotives, coaches, and wagons. In 1879, Werner von Siemens demonstrated the first practical electric locomotive at Berlin, a miniature locomotive that produced only three hp and carried passengers on a 300-meter-long train at about four miles an hour. Over the period 31 May–30 August 1879, 90,000 passengers rode this Siemens train. This led to exhibitions in 1881 at Brussels, Düsseldorf, and Frankfurt. A line was built from Lichterfelde outside Berlin a mile and a half long with a single electric car, and this became the first public electric railway in the world.

The first German-owned restaurant coach appeared in 1882, and the first corridor train also ran between Berlin and Cologne that same year. In 1883, there occurred the initial run of the now famous *Orient Express*. An electrical signaling block system debuted in Prussia in 1894, and two years later, Sunday railway tickets were introduced. In 1897, Wilhelm Schmidt designed the first super heaters for boilers. On 1 October 1899, the nation's first railroad museum opened—the Royal Bavarian Railway Museum—as Germany's oldest transport history showplace.

In 1902, the Berlin underground system opened, and five years later, there appeared a train ferry boat system between Germany and Sweden. In 1909, the Pfalzbahn was incorporated into the Bavarian State Railways, and the German Railway Wagon Association was founded as well. In 1910, the first modern freight car design was standardized and built, and the next year saw the first long-distance train electrification in Germany, from Bitterfeld to Dessau.

In 1912, the first Diesel locomotive was introduced, as well as the first all steel through-corridor express passenger coaches. On 24 November 1916—in the very middle of the First World War—the MITROPA Company was founded by different railroad companies in both Hohenzollern Imperial Germany and Habsburg Austria-Hungary, as an alternative to the *Compagnie Internationale des Wagonlits* of France, their wartime foe.

Following the loss of the war, CIWL (Wagon-Lits) took over most Central European passenger routes outside Germany. MITROPA maintained most of its routes within Germany, plus lines to The Netherlands and Scandinavia as well.

Military Railways, 1830–48

Starting in 1833, the military-political concept of strategic railways emerged, and by 1842, a full network of rail lines connected Germany to its future battlefronts—France in the west and Russia eastward. The French Chamber of Deputies at Paris took note officially of these "aggressive lines," correctly predicting that the "next" German invasion of France would come between Metz and Strasbourg.

In 1825, Friedrich Wilhelm Harkort of Westphalia—a Napoleonic Wars veteran—wrote an account of the British progress he had seen in railways and steamships. The next year, he set up a working model of a railway in the park of the Elberfeld Museum. In 1833, he pushed legislation in Westphalia to link the Weser and Lippe Rivers by rail. Later that same year, Harkort published *The Railroad from Minden to Cologne.*
This posited that, in future, large troop units could and would be deposited at concentration points much faster via rail than by the forced marches known since Roman times. It argued that both trains and the new telegraph communication lines would be sited together, and thus be capable of blocking the former French invasions of old over the Rhine River, the last being by Napoleon in 1806.

The year 1830 witnessed the appearance of British military railroads for the first time, as an army regiment rode the Liverpool–Manchester Line over 34 miles in two hours, a journey that previously took two full days on foot. Also, in 1842, the French Army started building its first track network of 900 miles that relied on its own national source of coal, iron, and steel in northern France, as well as on its native pool of trained engineers to run them.

Right from the start, telegraph lines were linked in tandem to railway development for communications. In 1842, German military writer Karl Eduard Pönitz praised Belgian railway progress made over that in Germany. While the German authorities martial at first ridiculed Harkort's ideas, in France the military aide to King Louis-Philippe saw their value. In 1846, the British War Office published an official report entitled, *Regulation Relative to the Conveyance of Her Majesty's Forces, their Baggage and Stores, by Rail.*

German critics in 1847 conceded that supplies, guns, and ammunition might, indeed, be transported by rail, but not troops, asserting wrongly that they would travel faster by marching, and also that even the best-organized line could not possibly transport 10,000 infantrymen over 60 English miles in 24 hours. They were to be proven dramatically wrong. That same year witnessed all manner of railroad lines crisscrossing the entirety of Continental Europe, supported by the heavy industrialized regions of the Rhineland, Silesia, and also northern and south-eastern France, plus large tracts of Habsburg Austria and the later Czech lands of 1919.

At the very core of the now fully emerging locomotive and railway industries were the later bane of conservative Germany, the politically leftist workers who themselves built them, their political views being asserted in their own well-read newspaper, *The Locomotive.*

Railways and the 1848–49 European Uprisings

By 1847, Prussian King Frederick Wilhelm IV needed money to pay for his railways, and thus called into session the United Diet to help raise it. When its members met, however, it called for liberal reforms that were anathema to the King, so he dissolved it that June. The following year, popular revolts broke out not only in Berlin—Prussia's capital—but also all across conservative Europe. Overthrown, Prince Klemens von Metternich of Austria fled Vienna by train, going into permanent exile, arriving in London on 21 April 1848. King Louis-Philippe's "July Monarchy" of 1830 was also overthrown in Paris in 1848, and soon the worried French authorities got the idea of sending resident Belgian rebels back to Belgium, also by rail, where they could be disarmed by the Belgian Army. Polish rebels resident in Germany were given free rail transport out of Germany, and back to Poland, an idea that Imperial Germany would reinvent in the Twentieth Century by giving Lenin free passage through the Second Reich into Tsarist Russia.

In the 1848 revolts within the embattled Kingdom of Prussia, ironically, the malcontents centered on the railroads, where the Social Democrats and Red Spartacists would again find their masses in 1918.

On 21 September, 1848, Berlin railway workers were urged to riot, and two of the military men who put these down later found fame and renown using railroads in the wars of 1864, 1866, and 1870–1: Gens. Friedrich von Wrangel (in 1864), and Helmuth von Moltke the Elder. "We now have 40,000 men in and around Berlin," stated von Moltke confidently. Gorlitz credited Moltke for his usage of railways and telegraphs.

The Berlin uprising occurred in mid-October, but on 10 November 1848, now Field Marshal von Wrangel entered the capital with 15,000 men and disarmed the rebels. The fighting nationwide continued, but by 5 May 1849, the Prussian uprisings were declared officially over. That same year, 30,000 Russian Army troops moved by rail from Poland to Moravia to put down revolts there. Rails had proven their worth in putting down rebellions, but not yet in war.

Military Railroading, 1846–59

During 1848–50, the Prussian Great General Staff in Berlin published a report entitled, *Survey of the Traffic and Equipment of German and of Neighboring Foreign Railways for Military Purposes*. Three years before, von Moltke—then a member of the General Staff—noted in a letter that while the French were *discussing* military railroads, the Germans were *building* them, at the rate of 3,300 miles of German railways to but a thousand for the French. Indeed, in 1846, Prussia's 6th Army Corps moved 12,000 men, horses, guns, road vehicles, and ammunition by rail on two lines to Krakow in Poland, the largest such movement to date of military forces by train.

In 1850, 75,000 Austrians with 8,000 horses and 1,000 vehicles were moved by rail from Vienna and Hungary to the Silesian frontier over 26 days and 150 miles. Despite single-line railways' shortcomings—not enough staff, lack of rolling stock, bad weather, poor planning, and restrictive transportation regulations—moved they *had* been nonetheless, a harbinger of things to come on a far more massive scale.

In 1851, Austrian railways transported an army division of 14,500 men with almost 2,000 horses, 48 guns, and 464 military vehicles 187 miles over two days from Kraków to Hradišt⬚, it being estimated that by marching, it would have taken 15 days. In 1853, martial writer Pönitz reported, "We have ... two fronts"—Russia in the east and France in the West. Troops had to arrive fresh at the end of their trip ready for action, with military railways as the best means of achieving that mission, he felt.

In 1853, Prussian military rail reforms began providing for the training of railroad non-commissioned officers and enlisted men, and by 1856, these forces had grown to full-sized railway battalions, linked to Army corps. In 1860, they became an independent arm of the Army, including an inspector-general, with each of the Army's nine corps having its own train battalion of 292 officers, NCOs, and enlisted personnel all wearing Regular Army uniforms.

Breakthrough for Railways Martial: The Italian Campaign of 1859

It was in Italy in 1859 during the Austro-French Italian War that military railways played their first real role in actual warfare, both strategically and tactically. Recalled a British military observer's official report in 1861, "By them, thousands of men were carried daily through France to Toulon, Marseilles, or the foot of Mont Cenis; by them, troops were hastened up to the very fields of battle; and by them, injured men were brought swiftly back to the hospitals, still groaning in the first agony of their wounds. "Moreover, the railway cuttings, embankments, and bridges presented features of importance equal or superior to the ordinary accidents of the ground, and the possession of which was hotly contested."

The 1859 Battle of Magenta was military history's first wartime railroad conflict, and even now the site can still be seen via the crosses marking where its soldiers fell, thus noting as well this initial deployment of railroad trains engaged in a vast military operation. In 1915, the contribution of the French military usage of trains to beat the Austrian Army at Magenta was again noted, with over 600,000 men and 120,000 horses deployed via railway across 86 days, without upsetting the normal, daily civilian side of rail traffic. There had been a daily average transit of 8,421 men with 512 horses, the very same private line also simultaneously running 2,636 civilian trains, as well as 236 military special trains. Indeed, fully 75,966 men and 4,469 horses had traveled via rail from Paris to the Mediterranean to the very borders of the Kingdom of Sardinia during 20–30 April 1859; a passage that would have taken two months of foot marching via road.

The estimated railway rate of travel was six times more over that of foot marches, or double as fast as the very best recorded German Army road travel up to then had been. Thus, the Imperial French Army of Emperor Napoleon III over-achieved as opposed to its future railroad rivals, the Germans. The food side of this rail equation fell short, however, as—of 25 June 1859—the day after the French had beaten their old, traditional enemy the Austrians in Italy—French soldiers for 24 hours had no food whatever, with their cavalry bereft also of fodder, resulting in no follow-up pursuit of the white-coated Austrians then in headlong retreat.

Emperor Franz Joseph of Austria in 1865.

Another negative aspect was that Gallic train efficiency was largely cancelled out by its military administration's ineptness; with 1859 being the preview of what followed 11 years later, in 1870. That, though, was on the far larger scale of the more momentous Franco-Prussian War that dragged on into 1871. Thus, railroads played a major role in the overthrow of Napoleon III after his crushing martial defeat at Sedan.

Nor did their beaten foes the Austrian Army learn from their 1859 mistakes. Their inept railway administration either delayed or entirely blocked Austrian troop trains, with stations becoming choked with much-needed supplies that never reached their intended destinations. The capital itself, Vienna, had a massive rolling stock shortage that grew even worse due to empty cars returning from the battlefield late, with even greater delays in sending fresh troops south to join the fighting in Italy, France's ally. Even then, however—when the troops finally arrived—the average complement so deployed was but a mere 360 men.

As with France herself in 1870, this boded ill for Austria-Hungary later on during the Six Weeks War with Prussia and Italy, but seven years hence. Meanwhile, at Berlin, Moltke studied the lessons of 1859 as well, but was far more influenced by the American Civil War. His developed concept of "marching separated, fighting united" was only made feasible by the advent of truly modern military railroading as it evolved in faraway North America.

The American Civil War as the First Full Railroad Struggle, 1861–65

It has been asserted that—as the sheer scale of the also known War of Secession and War Between the States covered a vast expanse of land—it could not have been waged at all without railroad warfare. Northern and Southern rival force separation was on a line of 2,000 miles, added to which were navigable canals, rivers, and maritime coastlines for both combatants, and yet it was the railways that took center stage in the final winning and losing of what has been called the first modern war, as we know that term today. The actual lines were somewhat primitive by our standards, being mostly single track over wooden bridges and rather shoddy ties. Still, many pitched battles were fought over the seizure of these very lines, communication hubs, and vital junctions. The South viewed its own lines as one of its main allies in its war against the Yankees.

The Union took control at the outset of the Philadelphia, Wilmington, and Baltimore Railway on 31 March 1861, and in January 1862, the Northern Federal Congress authorized President Abraham Lincoln

A railway mounted gun and its crew, used during the Siege of Petersburg in the American Civil War.

During their retreat from the Second Battle of Bull Run in the summer of 1862 Union soldiers destroyed trains and railroad tracks.

A mortar on rails. 1862 saw the creation of the United States Military Railroad. The USMR did not actually take over direct operation of the industry, but acted as its own enterprise and utilized private railroads when needed to offer the best tactical advantage for the military.

to seize whatever railroad and telegraph lines he deemed necessary for national security. A riot took place in April 1861 in Baltimore when Union troops passed from one station to another through the largely Secessionist town. Rocks and stones were thrown at the troops, who fired back, into the rioting crowd.

On 11 February 1862, U.S. Secretary of War Edwin McMasters Stanton issued a Federal order to seize all railroads on behalf of the Union: "Engines, cars, locomotives, equipments, appendages, and appurtenances." These were restored to their rightful civilian owners after the war, on 8 August 1865 by Executive Order. By that same 11 February 1862 order, Sec. Stanton appointed D. C. McCallum as Military Director and Superintendent of Railroads in the United States with the rank of brigadier general.

Over the full course of the Civil War, Union forces took 2,105 miles of rail lines, but—as also with the pair of German railroad wars in Russia—the greatest bane of American rail lines was gauge differences. It was not until the year after the end of the Civil War, in 1866, that all American railroad companies uniformly adopted the standard gauge of four feet eight-and-a-half inches for universal train line trackage.

In Russia later, though, the German Army was never able to overcome its own gauge dilemma, a major contributing factor to its loss of the Great War. The greatest problem other than gauge for both sides was shortages of engines, rolling stock, and rails, especially in the South, which lost the war.

The Civil War is now viewed as the first real scientific usage of military railways. Also revealed therein was the necessary establishment of an organized ground military railway engineer corps to operate, control, repair, restore, or destroy railroads on both sides of the fighting fronts. The Civil War also featured armored trains and the evolution of military

Railroads in the Civil War played a pivotal role in deciding how the campaign transpired. The North would hold a commanding advantage due not only to its industrial might (based in the Northeast) but also thanks to the heavy concentration of railroads operating from New England to the Midwest. The South also faced an additional problem, unforeseen when the conflict broke out; much of the fighting took place south of Virginia and as a result its railroads suffered tremendous damage as infrastructure—rails and telegraph—was disrupted or destroyed by Union forces.

Beginning in November of 1864, General Sherman led an overwhelming amount of soldiers from Atlanta to Savannah leaving a path of destruction. Railroad lines were destroyed, building burned to the ground, and livestock and crops were stolen.

United States Military Railroad 4-4-0 locomotive *W. H. Whiton* (built by William Mason in 1862) in January 1865 with Abraham Lincoln's presidential car.

ambulances, and even full hospital trains, for the first time. Outstanding military engineering successes were shown via the reconstruction of destroyed railroad bridges, and—as with industry—here again the North had an important edge over the agrarian South. This important Confederate railway disruption resulted in burned bridges and destroyed wooden ties, plus stolen rails that were then sent southward to the Confederacy halting Union troop reinforcement in the process.

The European military man who allegedly had best learned the martial railway lessons of that war was Gen. Helmuth von Moltke, Chief of the Prussian General Staff since 1857, but this was overstated. He did try to deploy them with but limited success in both of the latter two unification wars fomented by Prussia's Prime Minister von Bismarck during 1866–71, however.

The Austro-Prussian War with Denmark over Schleswig-Holstein, 1864

In 1859, Bismarck was appointed Prussian ambassador to the Russian Tsar at St. Petersburg, where he been stationed previously. By 1862, he was Prussian Prime Minister, serving under King of Prussia Wilhelm 1 (1797–1888). When Bismarck made his famous "blood and iron" speech about using martial means to effect Germany's unification, His Majesty took a train to fire him. Hastening to intercept him first, Bismarck met him at a deserted, unfinished railway station as King Wilhelm I changed trains—and got his desired reprieve.

At Berlin, meanwhile, von Moltke believed that a military railway could rapidly deploy the Prussian armies both east and west in any future conflict, as long as train schedule timetables were worked out in advance, this work being done in cooperation with the Ministry of Commerce, which at that time was responsible for the railway system. His first great rail transport exercises were held in 1862 in the Hamburg–Lübeck area, with a special view to a possible future war with Denmark.

Meanwhile, Bismarck's political unification plans hinged on a series of three wars, the first to detach the duchies of Schleswig and Holstein from neighboring, tiny Denmark. A temporary Prussian military alliance with rival Austria was made on 16 January 1864—as the American Civil War raged, unsettled—and thus kept the other Great Powers out of the duchies and Denmark. The two German allies marched into Schleswig on 1 February, with the new Prussian Crown Prince, Frederick Wilhelm, serving as second-in-command to Army Field Marshal von Wrangel, the first of the trio of struggles in which the Crown Prince would become a war hero. The war was soon over, with railways playing but a small part therein, though.

The Austro-Prussian-Danish War of 1864 did, however, provide von Moltke with the ideal testing opportunity to carry out his then martial railroading operational theories in actual battlefield practice. These included his prior 1861 adaptation of civilian railway coaches to transport non-severely wounded soldiers, with the more seriously injured men being placed instead in freight cars atop beds of straw, a practice later discarded.

Unfortunately for what he wanted to explore, though, this first war was but a limited, closed area, small-scale event, in which even the defending Danes themselves misunderstood the usage of their own rail lines, but not the attacking Prussians! Over the six-day period of 19–24 January 1864, Moltke deployed an entire army division of 15,000 men with 4,583 horses and 377 cars in 42 trains over the Minden-North Rhine West Line to Hamburg, some 175 miles distant, for an average of seven trains daily. In addition, supplies were also sent forward in February 1864 between Altona to Flensburg at two trains a day, as well as more sent north into Danish Schleswig. That, however, was the full extent of martial railroading in this small—but nonetheless important—war.

In general, this initial Prussian rail traffic war ran well, despite at least one known accident, with the mobile wooden ramps for unloading the trains being utilized rearward instead of sideways. As for the hapless Danes, their beaten army neglected to employ their Flensburg lines from Danewirk in Schleswig-Holstein but 21 miles away. Thus, their men

The aftermath of Battle of Dybbøl, the key battle of the Second Schleswig War which occurred on the morning of 18 April 1864 following a siege starting on 7 April. Denmark suffered a severe defeat against Prussia.

marched up to 18 hours rather than have a restful ride of a few hours before fighting tough rearguard actions with the pursuing Prussians, thereby losing in the process 600 men either killed in action or taken prisoners. The Danish military headquarters simply failed to grasp the railway lessons that Moltke had already taken to heart as much as he was able. In the end, Moltke deployed just under two full corps of 43,500 men, 100 guns, and 12,000 horses by rail, and even this figure was only a small part of his actual, available forces. The October 1864 Treaty of Vienna lost for Denmark the pair of contested duchies to the winning Prussian and Austrian Armies.

Moltke the Elder and the Six-Weeks Austro-Prussian War of 1866:

The First "German" Railway War
The second of Bismarck's unification wars was between the former 1864 allies, Austria and Prussia. They had last fought against each other during the Seven Years' War of Frederick the Great's era over the former Austrian province of Silesia, invaded and kept by the King. During the long French Revolutionary and then succeeding Napoleonic Wars, the two German-speaking nations had served together as common allies, but as 1866 approached, the issue was which of the two was to be supreme within

Germany overall? Von Moltke feared an Austrian assault on Berlin itself via Saxony, and so met this threat via a circular march into Habsburg Bohemia by way of Saxony and Silesia with four separate Prussian Army groups on the main Austrian Army concentration. In this grand invasion, he was greatly aided by the far superior Prussian mobilization system, as well as the rail grid necessary to see it through.

Numerically, von Moltke had five lines to Austria's one over almost 300 kilometers, with his ambitious scheme including that none of his men would unite until all units were in actual sight of the white-coated Austrian foe. This was on the previously designated battlefield, where six-sevenths of the entire blue-clad Prussians were earmarked for this singular, massive field gambit. What actually took place, though, on the Prussian railroad system was railhead confusion, with the required loading and unloading of forward troop supplies not made competently, with the still experimental stage mobile ramps not working out very well.

Surprisingly—even at the end of the wars of 1866 and 1870–71— another problem never really solved was that of clearing military railheads without their becoming too clogged with troops and supplies. Prussia's western defenses on the Rhine were to be denuded. Von Moltke gambled greatly and won, with railways playing a key transitional role.

Moving forward on a broad, 270-mile-wide front versus the Austrian Army were 250,000 Prussians, with von Moltke's strategy quickly beating both it and Vienna's ally, Saxony. An early proponent of railroads in war, in 1839 von Moltke had even become a board director of the

Helmuth Karl Bernhard von Moltke the Elder, (1800–1891), Field Marshal and the chief of staff of the Prussian Army for thirty years, he is regarded as the creator of a new, more modern method of directing armies in the field.

new Hamburg–Berlin line that he had partially funded via the Prussian War Ministry. Completely immersed in all matters technical of this new transportation modality, von Moltke's first prewar maneuvers were in 1859, as the Austrian Army attacked Piedmont. As Moltke wrote in 1843:

> Every new development of railways is a military advantage, and for the national defense, a few million on the completion of our railways is far more profitably employed than on our new fortresses!

In 1846, he deployed large-scale troop movements via rail. Administratively, von Moltke was able to put into practice what he had been preaching as well, indeed switching state funding to railways, and thus away from the static, stationary fortress building of yesteryear. Gradually, he subjugated many private railway companies under his wartime sway as well.

On the ground, therefore, he further ensured that all future railway construction occurred in areas of possible and even probable military usage someday—soon. Each of these new sites encompassed sidings and station platforms, plus rolling stock. In terms of communication, the man later known as "The Elder" was one of Continental Europe's first top commanders to send military orders and other "written" messages via electric telegraph wires, as opposed to the continued and obsolete usage of paper. From his Berlin headquarters, Moltke could direct his battles and campaigns personally via these new telegraph lines.

Indeed, his railway-supported "encirclement battles" were to become the hallmark of the later German victories in Russia and Poland during 1914–16. Ironically, von Moltke was partially undercut by his own Sovereign and military superior, King Wilhelm I of Prussia, who actually delayed the 1866 Prussian Army mobilization orders being issued, for fear of being accused of being the aggressor by public opinion. This, indeed, permitted the enemy Saxon Army via the Leipzig–Dresden Railway line's engines, passenger coaches, and freight cars to escape southeast, away from Moltke's pincers. Still, Moltke's overall successful deployment via the Prussian State Railway system rushed troops to the fighting front, and then evacuated the wounded men of both sides to military hospitals; in itself an historic military transit innovation.

Before his all-important, climactic, and decisive Battle of Königgrätz, Moltke also outmaneuvered the far slower Austrian railway service by deploying along his own trio of lines the Prussian Army forward. Conversely, the Saxon Army burned the Riesa railway bridge and blew up Meissen's stone structure to help slow the Prussian juggernaut. Counter to that, the Prussians' seizure of Saxon rolling stock greatly enabled Moltke's occupation of the Kingdom of Saxony itself, thus knocking it out of the brief war altogether. But not without a struggle, as Saxon Army trainmen from top to bottom started a retrograde movement to protect their Royal treasury from falling to Prussia.

On 18 June 1866 from Riesa and Chemnitz to Zwickau, Prussian cavalry was dispatched to abort its escape to the allied Bavarian frontier, but failed. This precipitate flight was even joined *en route* as Saxon trains going north reversed themselves and headed south instead, this gambit being repeated at all stations along the way, too. Whether full, empty, or half-full, all such cars were quickly uncoupled and reset, rapidly sliding away from a Prussian enemy hot in pursuit. At Reichenbach, there was seen the extra spectacle of several trainloads in quick succession—including sometimes as many as six engines both fired up and not—coming *en route* straight from their own locomotive sheds in rear areas. That night at Eger Station, there was assembled a vast, saved array of Saxon rolling stock: 140 locomotives and nearly 8,000 cars at this, Saxony's last rail network location. A second exodus to Austrian Army-controlled Hungary took place a few days later. During 19 June–November 1866, therefore, only Prussian Army trains traversed the entire conquered Saxon state.

The Prussian armies duly surrounded the Austrians on 3 July 1866 at the famous Battle of Königgrätz, in which Crown Prince Frederick Wilhelm again shone as Prussia's hero; 34,000 Austrian, Saxon, and Prussian troops were killed, and many more wounded, in this bloody, single day's combat. Amazed military observers worldwide were agog at the speedy deployment of the Prussian Army on Saxony's own service lines via that

Emperor Friedrich III (1831–1888) photographed when he was Crown Prince Frederick William of Prussia.

same Leipzig–Dresden line and ever onward. The war ended in August 1866 when Austria signed Prussian-imposed peace terms at Prague, where was also formed Bismarck's new North German Confederation that excluded beaten Vienna, with Saxony becoming as well victorious Prussia's newest acquired vassal state.

This same Six Weeks War witnessed also Prussian Army anti-civilian population terrorist retaliation operations for attacks on its lines that were to become thereafter a highlight of all future German wars, too. Asserted military observer Capt. Webber:

> The Prussians were fortunate in being able to preserve the line intact from injury by the inhabitants—partly by the number and strength of the guard posted along it—and partly from the terror of reprisals that they had inspired....

Webber's eyewitness report was published two years after the war, entitled, *Notes on the Campaign in Bohemia in 1866.* Such "terror reprisals" would occur again, during the war of 1870–71, and even more during the Great War, too.

Another key factor had been that Prussia had mobilized all her forces within a mere three weeks, whereas it took the Austrians fully six; von Moltke's belief in, and usage of, railways had, indeed, paid off, handsomely in this regard. On 6 May 1866, Moltke had wisely created his Prussian Field Railway Section, the won war against Austria and her allies fully having justifying his prudent action.

On 5 May 1867, King Wilhelm I approved the new, secret *Route Service Regulation*—also adopted by the other German states over time. It created a special Railway Department of the Prussian General Staff for the first time, and also, a Railway Field Corps, charged with maintaining vital lines of communication: roads, highways, bridge crossings, telegraph wires, and postal usage, all enabling as well Prussian governance of its new enemy lands, all major steps forward in military railroading. Next came a District Line Commissioner, the concept of railheads and halting places, an Inspector General of Communications, a Director of Field Railways, and more formalized route inspection, too. One ruler who watched with alarm the lessons of the 1866 campaign was Emperor Napoleon III of France, but not enough to order the necessary radical reforms in obsolete French railway practices, though.

In retrospect, it was seen that von Moltke's Prussian Railway Service had been thusly deployed as war broke out in 1866: the mobilization of a trio of corps' divisions of Railway Troops, each of the Army's three separate armies being assigned one, and all operational in a different

Louis-Napoléon Bonaparte (1808–1873), nephew of Napoleon I, President of the French Second Republic (1848–52) and, as Napoleon III, Emperor (1852–70) of the Second French Empire. The French army was rapidly defeated in the Franco-Prussian War of 1870 and Napoleon III was captured at the Battle of Sedan. The French Third Republic was proclaimed in Paris, and Napoleon went into exile in England.

wartime theater sector of its own as well. These Railway Troop Divisions had both military and civilian components, with engineer officers manning the martial section, and non-commissioned officers plus enlisted carpenters and blacksmiths in elite pioneer sections. They were joined by engine drivers, foremen, and skilled machinists, the latter responsible for repairing broken water pumps and tanks, the all-important engine motive power drivers, and the rolling stock pulled by them.

The Austrian Army in turn attacked with a vengeance the steamroller-like Prussian Army forward movement, via the destruction of viaducts and bridges, torn up rails, burned out sleepers, stolen turntables and points, blocked tunnels, and disabled water pumps and cranes to boot. Only "Six Weeks" the war may have been, but it was no cakewalk for the Prussian Army. Planted Austrian Army anti-railway mines brought down heavy rock formations onto the rails below, and obstructed cuttings. In addition, the rocks could not be moved away until broken down into smaller parts, and thus cleared by Prussian Army engineers' explosive detonations in turn. Using ballast trucks to haul off this impedimenta of modern war, Prussian engineers deployed 50 pioneers and 20 workers, clearing the blocked lines before midnight of that very day's earlier wastage by the Austrians.

Despite von Moltke's having studied the errant French Army's railway errors of 1859, seven years later, the Prussian Army repeated many of them nevertheless. Planned-for unloading at supposed forward rail depots did not occur, and these then stationary freight cars also clogged both railway stations and sidings, as well as not being re-routed elsewhere. Both Moltke and his subordinate commanders were also and surprisingly completely ignored as local field leaders issued their own direct orders to the railway men within their individual, jurisdictional fiefdoms instead, thus creating in turn disconnected operating lines in their domains. Postwar, Moltke and his planners sought to remedy this train chaos with the establishment of the General Staff Line of Communications Department, plus a Central Commission, the latter a civilian-military body to oversee all future wartime railway deployments.

A Construction and Destruction Corps was also created within the Prussian Army, as well as an Operation Corps to both destroy and restore railways in time of war. A Prussian Royal Decree of 10 August 1869 by His Majesty the King upgraded the permanent leadership corps of the Railway Troop pioneers trained overall in railway operations, building, and destruction for the next war in 1870. This included an operations corps to both destroy and restore railways in wartime. During 1871, there was raised in addition a new pioneer battalion, the latter not copied by the much smaller British Army until 1882.

Still—and despite all its Six Weeks War shortcomings—until 29 June 1866, Prussian military trains advanced with their troops, then got left in the rear until after Königsgrätz decided the war for good. During this vital campaign—as "efficient" Prussian troops found themselves snarled in huge traffic jams—the soldiers already at the front fought on, taking their own shelter and food where they found both, or simply did without. Surprisingly—and especially in this so-called Railway Age—Moltke's Prussian Army began mobilizing after the Austrian Army, then being forced to make up for lost time via deployment along all five of its frontier destination train lines. It was this, therefore, that created the myth of Moltke's later famed "strategy of external lines," along an arc extending over 200 miles in troop deployment more than anything else. An unmeant stratagem, Moltke's supposed gambit was, in reality, nothing more than his reaction to this unplanned for accident, rather than due to now over-famed Prussian "planning."

Moltke's response, therefore, was conditioned by the railway logistical concerns of 1866 and thereafter, all the way into the autumn of 1918: space, time, and the physical layout of the Prussian State Railway system. Thus, Moltke's 1866 railway mobilization was not the complete success of later historical mythology, but worked nonetheless, with 197,000 men and 55,000 horses moved in 5,300 cars in but 21 days, or three weeks. Once arrived at their designated railheads, however, they soon found themselves sometimes blocked from reaching the front, this being caused by congestive, snarled backups. Indeed, it was estimated as June 1866 ended, that at least 17,920 supply tonnage was, in fact, stranded immobile on its own lines, with both forward and rear motion impossible. "Hundreds" of immobilized railway cars instead served as ersatz magazines, being kept static in place even had the lines been open on which to move them.

Stale bread, rotted horse fodder, and dead cattle slain by malnutrition forced Moltke's forward field commanders to simply operate without the later so-called railway miracle at hand. All communication and linkage between forward troop elements and the now rearward railways was completely severed, with the hard driving foot soldiers having, therefore, out-foot-marched their allegedly "faster" rolling stock! The stunning, resultant fact was, therefore, that from the first crossing of 23 June 1866 and the all-vital Battle of Königsgrätz—Moltke's cherished trains had no influence on how the campaign was actually won. In addition, it further galled the victorious onsite ground commanders that they were unable even to use the captured Austrian Army trains to pursue their beaten foe. This was due to their own system's breakdown caused by incompetence, and also—admittedly—the usual unforeseen circumstances of all wars.

As the stationary Austrian fortress works at Königstein, Theresien, Josefstadt and Königgrätz stood astride the railway's path to Barduwitz of their projected advance to Vienna, the ground force commanders simply acted as if the enemy fortresses did not exist. They marched past them, and on to the vulnerable Habsburg capital until war's end—and Bismarck's conclusion of peace—halted them in their tracks. In this light, these mighty forts did not exist!

In his famous postwar letter to Bismarck of 6 August 1866, Moltke made a few key points: minor damage to the railways was soon repaired, with only the pesky Austrian fortresses hindering their men's advance. Still, "It was with rails, not brickwork, that the future lay," the old soldier firmly believed. The fact remained, however, that he had to do better with his railways in the next war. By 1859, the French railway system was already far superior to those of Prussia and Germany, so this would be no mean feat, he felt.

At the 1866 war's beginning, all three of the Prussian Army's Railway Divisions had its separate repair train, equipped with an engine at both ends front and rear; this being preceded on track by a four-man-propelled hand trolley led by an officer with a bugler for audio communication. This latter worthy alarmed the following repair train as and when blockage was sighted, with the dispatch of hardy pioneers to remove, repair, or both. If attacked, the repair train's rear engine pulled it away to safety and reinforcements.

Moltke's subsequent military reputation as the war's greatest strategist was , in fact, saved by its first and only major conflict, that at Königgrätz, where his adjusted, dispersed army strategy succeeded almost by accident, with the resultant smashing victory winning for him military history's now recognized laurels. And this in spite of the complete lack of Prussian pursuit via rail—the very opposite of what Blücher had achieved in the days after Waterloo 51 years earlier—right up to and including Paris in 1815, both on foot and horseback. Seen in this negative aspect, it was as if railroads had never been invented. It was even more galling to the entire Prussian Army from the King down to the lowliest private that Bismarck's high politics of reconciliation with today's defeated Austrian foe as tomorrow's stalwart ally, forbade any triumphant entry into their capital. For their part, the Austrians were worse than the Prussians in their usage of what railways they had, and failed to totally destroy them in the path of the advancing Prussians as well. They also left important rolling stock behind, as at Prague, for the Prussians to capture and use. Their inept railway administration either delayed or entirely blocked Austrian Army troop trains, with stations thus becoming clogged and even blocked completely with much needed supplies that never reached their intended destinations.

Railroad War Supreme? The Franco-Prussian War of 1870–71

Bismarck's diplomacy had been successful during his first two "wars of unification" in that all of the Great Powers save the combatants had stayed neutral—especially France in the west, and Russia in the east. Thus, there was no "two-front war" such as bedeviled the Wilhelmine Reich during 1914–18. In 1870, however, he was forced to take on the Imperial France of Emperor Napoleon III, but again Russia—and now also England—remained neutral, permitting Prussia to unite Germany into a great, new German Second Reich. Great Britain had not been a presence on the Continent since 1815, while tsarist Russia appreciated the fact that Prussia had stayed neutral during her own Crimean War with France and Britain during 1853–54, and now returned the favor.

On 16 July 1870, Prussia mobilized again, for the third time in 10 years. With the rapid Prussian Army occupation of conquered French territory, it was forced to post at all captured railway stations formations of German *Landwehr/Militia,* with smaller units placed as well in surrounding villages and towns, to protect their own lines of communication back to Germany. Troops were also left at all signal boxes, and at three-four-mile intervals over the entire French railway system to patrol it. This encompassed 100,000 protective troops along 2,000 miles of French lines,

Above and Right: Prussian Army troops entrain for France, 1870. *Library of Congress*

Prussian soldiers on their way to the front, 1870.

and then—even still!—the dreaded enemy *franc-tireur* saboteurs caused great damages.

Prussian observers from the American Civil War period simply copied in Occupied France what they had seen the Union Army do in America: force top French citizens from each occupied area to be passengers on all Prussian engines in France as a visual deterrent against such attacks. Conversely, a single French peasant terrorist could and did put hundreds of German rail riders' lives in mortal jeopardy simply by placing a heavy stone on a line, or taking away a single rail.

During 1870–71, there were fully 51 agencies controlling 15 Prussian State Railway Directorates, five of these being private civilian lines, although state-run anyway; and another 31 company-operated completely private railroads, all running but 210 miles of each line.

Armored trains were deployed during the ground fighting of the 1870 war, as well as for the stalemated Siege of Paris that lasted into January 1871 when the city surrendered. In four separate instances, these armored locomotives took to the field, their having been constructed at the French Orleans company: armor-plated cars with gun mounts affixed, overhead protective coverings made of five wrought iron plates two fifths of an inch thick apiece. In addition, the pair of locomotives used had their own armor plating. The few cars that were struck by enemy field gun fire resulted only in but partially dented plating, with both the engine and cab being entirely unscathed in the melee. These Prussian armored trains were each followed into combat by secondary armored engines carrying pioneer mechanics equipped with both repair materials and the requisite tools, especially necessary when it came time to withdraw from the front. On the initial outing, however, the repair crews were engaged for about 15 minutes in such work.

Again as in 1866, so, too, was it in 1870 not Moltke's entirely successful railway mobilization over nine concentrated lines: six for the Northern Army and three for the Southern deployed over the course of 24 July–3 August 1870. Thereon, a total of 1,200 troop trains transported 350,000 men; 87,000 horses, and 8,400 guns, all but only slightly hampered by delays, though. Thus—by 5 September 1870—five separate rail lines held static 2,322 cars of 16, 830 tons of Prussian 2nd Army supplies for 26 days' worth of combat field operations. This meant both a scarcity of more needed wagons, plus rearguard French Army line destruction in their retreat, all of which stymied their timely Prussian and now also German railway delivery.

The French, however, had even greater difficulties, with the Emperor Napoleon III himself arriving at Metz to take personal command, only

A French hospital train, 1870.

French railway wagons used as a mobile hospital, 1870.

to find his 2nd Army in confusion on the 14th full day of mobilization. Indeed, in the face of the surging German armies crossing into France, the Emperor had at hand only 200,000 out of an expected 350,000 soldiers actually with their designated units, and even these were lacking basic gear and clothing such as uniforms. In addition, many Reserve soldiers due to report in were simply missing *en route*, instead fighting and drinking in public, and whoring, as they "sought" their regiments to fight the Germans, with more stranded at railway depots as well. The very same was also true of their missing supplies, as the French railway system clogged, choked, and then halted in place. When they did arrive at their correct destinations, they could still not be unloaded, for want of the necessary facilities and crews. All of this resulted in pre-combat dissolution of French discipline, causing amateur soldier Napoleon III to be the first to realize that the Germans might be able to strike first, and thus win, as occurred. The Emperor's own railway travel seemed to mirror the disarray in the French military railroad system overall. The waiting "Imperial" train at Verdun was an embarrassment: a substandard engine pulling a third class coach for His Majesty, and a pair of cattle cars for his august entourage.

From Berlin, Moltke had already guessed the French Army's weak points, bypassed its vaunted frontier fortresses, and drove on instead to fight the main Gallic field armies with a trio of Prusso-German Army groups on his own five designated lines. Whereas Moltke's generally efficient rail section timed railway movements with precision wherever possible—"The Elder" even supplying Bismarck with a personal copy of the scheduled movements— incredibly the French Army began the 1870 campaign without same. Thus, the French instead depended upon a shaky mixture of both military and private railway schedules. In 1869, the late French Army Marshal Nie wanted to militarize all French railroads in time of war, as well as complete his own rail lines from Verdun to Fortress Metz, but died a month following his plan's introduction. Moreover, Nie's successor reversed those concepts, bowing as well to the civilian political clout of the Minister of Public Works at Paris.

At first, French Army units duly departed from Alsace-Lorraine in a timely fashion, but the follow-up infantry battalions, cavalry squadrons, and artillery batteries all found themselves stalled in a mass railway car traffic jam—just as had bedeviled Moltke himself in 1866. Since then, the Prussian Army had developed six "strategic railways" of either fully or partially double tracked industrial and population center trunk lines to the Rhine River. Of these six, three covered north and central Germany from Berlin, the remaining trio with one each from Munich, Hamburg, and Dresden in Germany. By contrast, the French Army boasted but four such: Paris–Sedan–Thionville, Paris–Metz–Forbach, Paris–Nancy–Hagenau, and Belfort–Strasbourg, with the vital fifth—Verdun–Metz—incomplete. Also left undone was the double track connecting lines for Thionville–Forbach, Strasbourg, and Hagenau that would have joined the four French railways together.

Whereas the Prussian Army relied mainly on double track lines, the French had mostly single tracks going but one way. This resulted in 1870 with the Germans transporting 50 trains daily on average to the French frontier, with the French left far behind with but a mere dozen only. Even worse, the French Army trains could move but a single infantry battalion, cavalry squadron, artillery unit, or supply column on any one of its trains, thus using up three full weeks of precious time to assemble a solitary army group that took the Prussians only three to seven days. On 27 July 1870, a British journalist at Metz reported:

> You cannot conceive the difficulty of uniting even 100,000 men! Sometimes 30 wagons roll into the station and—after all the equipment had been taken off—just 50 men step down!

This dichotomy also occurred on a far greater scale regarding a full field army of multiple corps, with trains left stationary at sidings in expectation of missing units arriving; supplies thus unloaded and given to units in place, standing idle, and all this miles away from their designated railheads.

Chaos reigned supreme thereby, forcing the French main eastern Paris–Forbach line to close down altogether; cars simply could not be unloaded quickly enough on the trunk lines to maintain functioning for a full day in July's third week so as to reassemble along the line all the missing troops, horses, guns, food, ammunition, and ambulances, and then count, collect, and reorganize them for re-embarkation.

Moltke's staff by comparison had achieved this in 1868 in all 13 of the Prussian Army corps, with specific tracks posted for them, the same being true as well for Prussia's allied south German divisions, with timetables and concentration locales decided upon well in advance. Prussia began its 1870 campaign with the former four sections of railway troops ramped up to six that included a single allied Bavarian Army unit, too. Each of these sections' troops sported an *E* on their uniform shoulders that stood for *Eisenbahntruppen* (railroad troops), and all were armed with rifles for combat if necessary as well: engineers, pioneers, railway men, and auxiliary helpers. Stunningly, the French Army had no such railway troops. Still, once their retreat within France herself began, the French Army proved itself to be a far more destructive force than had been the Austrian four years earlier. This forced the German Army to rebuild its main

Paris–Strasbourg line for the future siege of the French capital during 17 September–22 November 1870. Meanwhile, French troops exploded six mines to block the Nanteuill Tunnel's west end with collapsed walls, and three-and-four-square yards of sand. Between Nancy–Toul at Fontenoy-sur-Moselle, the French failed to destroy, though, a seven-arched bridge with mid-passage explosions. Only a single pair was brought down instead on a side, thus allowing German sappers to merely fill it in with rocks and earth. Several French-mined Vosges Mountain tunnels were emplaced with faulty mines, with the Germans thus able to seize them still intact before orders to detonate arrived. Indeed, French civilian partisans had a better record than the regular French Army who—on the Meuse River alone—derailed a full Prussian troop train.

Despite such sabotage, the Germans managed to operate 2,500 kilometers of French railway lines that they occupied, but 3,500 more railway men had to be sent from Germany into France, in addition to the German railway troops already there.

As the war was being decisively won by Prussia and her German allies, the new German Empire was proclaimed in the Hall of Mirrors at Versailles in January 1871. On 19 May, a Royal Order stipulated that the Prussian Army as of 1 October would have a new railway battalion to encompass all railroad duties that had been found so necessary during the late war. The Bavarian Army also acquired one in December 1872, as part of the new overall Federated Army of the German Empire.

Overall, 400,000 Prussian-German Army troops had reached the front within the first 18 days of mobilization, while the French Army had sent their men to depots first, and not directly to the front—another crucial error. Moltke's surprise victory over the Austrians—and Bismarck's 1867 establishment of the North German Confederation—had brought Prussia additional military forces. All of this allowed "The Elder" to abandon his earlier projected defensive war with France behind the Rhine, and instead pivot over onto an offensive stance in 1870. In addition, Moltke in 1867 had realized that any future effective war against France hinged on the construction of ever more railway lines upon which to bring completely into play his new North German Confederation alliance martial units. Conferring with Prussian War Minister Gen. Albrecht von Roon, Moltke was authorized to build what he wanted most: four more lines on which to mass the 13 North German army corps in four weeks rather than six. At war's outset, Col. von Brandenstein was commanding officer of rail transit and supply, with but a pair of direct lines Germany–Paris. One—the furthest north—was confronted by French forts astride his path via Reims, Sedan, and Metz, to be either destroyed or bypassed. Another was blocked by Fortress Toul until 23 September 1870 through Châlons-sur-Marne,

Francs-tireurs in the Vosges, 1870.

An 1870 photograph, one of the very first taken of a battle. It shows a line of Prussian troops advancing at the Battle of Sedan, 1 September 1870. The photographer was standing with the French defenders when he captured this image.

Bar-le-Duc, Nancy, and Lunéville, all important French urban areas. The 1870 campaign began as well with Prussian freight cars clogging their own lines, with the most fortunate capture of French provisions saving the invading German forces from actual starvation. Here again in 1870—as in 1866 before—it was railway line blockage by unloaded freight cars rushed forward anyway, without any facility for unloading them at the end. They simply choked off the overworked railway line routes in the event.

In addition at Metz—where the cars could have been unloaded—they just were not, due to rampant confusion regarding where they were to go if they were. In the end, the entirety of the "efficient" Prussian Army railway system remained choked to a standstill, and therefore static and unloaded on sidings once more, unable to be sent on ahead to the very places most necessary. Being full, these very same cars could not be unloaded, and were twice over redundant. The Prussians never solved this dilemma, either, whereas the French did not know they had the same problem until after their defensive war was already hopelessly lost. On both sides, moreover—as their cars were even freed up—neither had ready to hand the necessary crews to run them, and were minus necessary rolling stock as well. Unable to dragoon French railway men, the Germans had to bring in 3,500 of their own to run the 50 captured French locomotives. The latter necessitated the Reich sending forward 280 more engines, with both dislocation and shortages on the rear side domestic front as a result.

Ironically, as the 1870 campaign opened, the French Army's completed internal lines did not prevent their being completely defeated anyhow. French Army lines ran parallel with the Reich's western frontier, thus tying together their border forts as well, while all the German lines ran north to south instead. As late as 1856, Prussian Prince Wilhelm—then commander-in-chief of the Prussian Army—was against building military lines on the Rhine, but both he and Moltke changed their minds later on.

Post-1871 Reforms

During 1870–99, the chief of the now German Great General Staff also became the new inspector general of the railway battalion, upgraded to a full regiment on 30 December 1875, and was expanded again in 1890 to a brigade of two regiments. On 25 March 1899—united together as communications troops—were all railway technical units, telegraphic, and, later, aircraft services, placed under a general of division reporting directly to His Majesty Kaiser Wilhelm II, King of Prussia and German Emperor.

During 1879–1902 under the new Second Reich of the Kaisers, state railway ownership increased from 6,300 kilometers to 31,000. Rolling stock on these same state lines increased as follows: locomotives from 7,152 to 13,267; passenger cars from 10,828 to 24,225; and freight cars from 148,491 to 303,364.

In retrospect, the later common view crediting the Prussian rail lines mainly with the defeat of the French was clearly wrong; to the contrary, the Prussians seemed to have won the war despite their better railroads. The initial line Prussian Army blockage we have seen was in place as early as 3 August 1870, and thus Moltke's later much-touted efficiency made a mockery of, for the second time since 1866. In addition to that, it was not until 25 September 1870 that the powerful French Army fortress chain was overcome, by which time the other war of ground troop movement had already won the war, without the railways. Thus—even as King Wilhelm I's armies were marching on Paris—behind them complete train chaos continued, with lines clogged for literally hundreds of miles behind the front, static trains sitting all the way back into Germany as far as Cologne and even Frankfurt. The statistics are simply staggering: by 5 September 1870, on five separate lines sat 2,322 full freight cars with 16,830 tons of non-used supplies for the 2nd Army alone, in what was then the campaign's projected second phase.

Prussian cavalry had been ordered to capture as much French railway rolling stock as possible, as well as locomotives. In 1870—as in 1914—French *franc-tireur* saboteurs slowed down the Prussian railway steamroller in combat operations. French Army Marshal François Achille

Napoleon III and Bismarck talk after Napoleon's capture at the Battle of Sedan.

Bazaine surrendered Metz fortress on 9 September 1870, the ring was then closed around Paris, and the English Channel was reached by December; the French fort at Belfort held out until the very end of the war in 1871, however.

Fully 2,000 miles of French railway track was used by the German armies during the war, and—for the first, but not the last, time—French hostages were placed on the front of locomotives to deter the trains being blown up. Rails were essential at only two points during the war: at the outset concerning initial troop deployment *en masse,* and then again at the end, during the protracted Siege of Paris, in which the Germans bombarded the city with heavy artillery. The trains were then necessary to bring up both the guns and their ammunition.

Von Moltke has been blamed for these failures of the German military rail system, and it has been alleged that he spent the rest of his career of 25 years covering up his mistakes in the bright blaze of martial glory that helped to obscure them. The four German armies in France were forced to live off the land, as they would do again in 1914. The longest distance from the furthest forward railhead to the front was, in fact, 130 miles by November 1870. As three German armies concentrated on Paris, their railroads were being destroyed by the French. Indeed, the invaders' supply situation was so critical that the Siege of Paris was actually delayed for two months while German soldiers helped French civilians bring in the fall harvest to feed them all, and also to stockpile the necessary heavy artillery ammunition with which to bombard the surrounded French capital once the infamous siege actually started. Not only could German trains not defend themselves from enemy assault, but adjacent Prussian Army unit commanding officers could have cared less whether or not they survived. Their war was being won on foot and horseback as in the past, and not by the trains of the future.

Oddly, in fact, Moltke had learned none of the lessons of 1866, with later historians granting him a prescience of expected martial accomplishment that was totally misplaced in the actual event. Thus, the freight loading and unloading dilemma only worsened in 1870, and this was especially true as well regarding the troops at key transfer points. Plus, there were never enough *E* men to safeguard their own lines, nor was any central railroad headquarters ever established. Without enough crews to unload them, rations by the millions just rotted away in place, their designated troops never receiving them. Likewise, chaos existed, too, within Prussian Army and German Army communications organizations. Problems at the war's outset simply persisted right until the war's end—unsolved. Even though 100 tons daily on six-seven trains would have sufficed, they never arrived; nor were Prussian railway troops alone able to take the sturdy

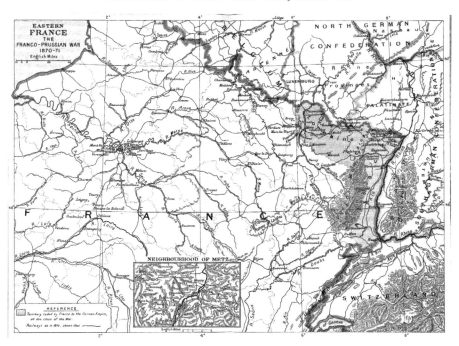

A map of the Franco-Prussian War showing the railway lines in existence in 1870.

A German ammunition train *c.* 1870.

The Champs-Elysees in 1871, following the siege of Paris.

French forts blocking the rail right of passage. Bypassed and left utterly fallow in the German rear areas, the untaken French forts continued to hamper the German communication lines for the front all the way back to Berlin. Oddly—and in this way—the losing French railway system ended the war in a more positive stance than did the winning Prussian Army's; nonetheless, ever since, Moltke has won the rail war according to inaccurate historians.

On a higher plane, though, the Franco-Prussian War did inaugurate the Age of Coal and Steel. In retrospect, the same loading and unloading dilemma confronted all the same European armies once more in 1914. Despite the fact that 117 trains could move a full army corps along 600 miles of double track in but nine days, it remained uneconomical over just 100 miles due to the still unresolved dispersal problem for large units of all arms. This was in spite of the fact that—24 years after 1870—European railroads encompassed 65,000 track miles, an increase of 200 percent. The two Continental powers with the largest ground forces—the new Second Reich and the old tsarist Muscovy—enjoyed even greater percentages. Also, by 1914, each line could transport an estimated 40 trains daily on a single track, and 60 on double, increases over 1870 of eight and twelve respectively.

With 1870–71 being accorded by historians as the first and sole railway war of the Nineteenth Century in Europe, the rival national lines were estimated to be about roughly equal, with France having the fifth most dense on earth, and Prussia the fourth, but still it was the German east–west lines that were pronounced the most important. While the Prussian Army had as well its east–west *Ostbahn* (east railway) line to carry troops to and from the northeast, the new "Germans" since 1867 displayed deep-rooted coordination problems via their widely disparate train and railway practices. This was partially due to the Reich having been a single, unitary state only since 1871, or for about 43 years total, as 1914 opened; a political fact often noted by the third and last German Kaiser himself. The Saxon railway minister offered rather cattily that it would be:

> To the general good in peacetime—and of benefit to the military man in wartime—if the superintendent met at Cologne [on the Rhine] was dressed like the superintendent at Königsberg [East Prussia], and if there was no danger of a Hamburg station inspector being taken for a superintendent of the line by somebody from Frankfurt.

The above were very astute observations, indeed. Moreover, he archly added that:

> There were parts of the network on which a white light meant 'stop,' and others where it signified 'all clear,' a real risk to the safety of people traveling on the system.

Surprisingly, although von Moltke the Elder's "line commissions" of the Prussian General Staff Center at Berlin were in place as the 1870 gamble commenced, it was instead from Paris that a thousand trains over three weeks had carried 300,000 men and 65,000 horses plus guns, supplies, and ammunition. This was despite all their previous shortcomings, moreover, and remarkably, 86,000 soldiers over 10 days had reached the Franco-German frontier first, finding fewer Prusso-German forces opposite to fight them. Even so, the overall French railway system was rotten at its core, despite the above impressive statistics, hiding as they did both incompetence and a disorganization that beset the overall French war effort from start to finish. Indignantly, one French general noted bitterly postwar that:

> You could see your railway trains encumbered by men crisscrossing their way in all directions—and in all parts of France—often arriving at their destinations just when the corps to which they belonged had left, then running after this corps, only to catch it up when it was beaten, in retreat, or besieged in an inaccessible fortress!

At the French Army fortress at Metz, the local civil populace was nonetheless impressed with what it nicknamed *the Iron Cross Railway:* with 4,000 men constructing a 22-mile ring using captured French material to lay siege to both the fort and the city. In strict railroad terminology, it was not an engineering marvel, having steep inclines that could hold but three-four cars on a single train, with derailments being caused by overly sharp curves. In spite of its downsides, *the Iron Cross Railway* displayed German planning and intensity at their most thorough to the amazed natives anyway. Indeed, 400,000 German soldiers reached the front in the first 18 days of overall mobilization over nine lines, but they were not used in the advance on Paris after the Battle of Sedan virtually decided the outcome of the entire campaign in September 1870. Oddly, von Moltke had planned initially to fight the war on German territory—and not in France at all—and thus planned to use only Prussian railways, and not French.

The most influential railway memoir of the war was published by French author François Jacqmin, entitled, *The Railways During the War of 1870–71,* in which he wrote that:

> There had to be a unified control of the railways for military purposes, whether it was the transport of troops or supplies, and ... there had to be a 'permanent association' of the military and technical elements ... a joint command that would ensure ... smoother operations in practice approaching the battlefields.

When the Prussian–German armies simply stopped in place, railroads once more became irrelevant regarding re-supply of the forward areas. It even transpired that fighting ceased altogether, so that peasant-origin German troopers could strip off their field jackets to help local French farmers harvest their crops so that none would starve during the coming winter of 1870–71. This has been termed as, "The last time in history that an army would carry out such a function." Meanwhile, both the French people at the time—and historians since—have put the blame for losing the war on the abdicated Emperor of the French Napoleon III and his Spanish-born aristocratic Empress Eugenie. After Sedan, the Imperial regime at Paris was overthrown by a rioting Parisian mob, in concert with French politicians, the latter replacing the Second—and thus far last—French Empire with the Fifth French Republic.

As for the winning side in 1871, the Prusso–Germans—prior to many more modern historians—took the mistaken view that not only had railroads won the war, but also that the side that had the best and used them first in the attack would always win. Little was reformed. In contrast, the calamity on the French railways led to major reformation right up to 1914. Both sides ramped up rail construction also, significantly adding to the political tension that led to the First World War. Some historians have argued that—had the two Moltkes not drawn their wrong railroad conclusions, and admitted to themselves that the 1871 victory was due more to French mistakes than to Prussian transit genius— the First World War might not have played out as it did. Instead, Prusso–German military doctrine insisted on a strike first mantra that would "guarantee" victory in the field to the side that did.

Regarding losses, there were 180,000 casualties of both killed in action and wounded for both sides inclusive over the course of the 10-month-long struggle during which the main fighting was over within the first six. Thus, the first European railway war set the stage for the next

2

Kaiser Reich, 1871–1914

A New 99-Day Reign Begins with a Train Ride, 1888

On 10 March 1888, the new German Emperor—Kaiser Frederick III (the second having been Frederick the Great)—left a sickbed at the Villa Zirio at San Remo, Italy by special train to return to his native Prussia, where he was now also its King. Accompanying him was the new German Empress and Queen of Prussia, Kaiserin Viktoria, formerly Princess Royal of Great Britain, eldest daughter of Queen Victoria.

Their route would be over the Brenner Pass via Munich to Chartlottenburg, just west of Berlin. The stricken monarch succeeding his dead father was himself already dying from inoperable throat cancer, and wrapped around his doomed neck was a broad wool scarf to ward off the bitter German cold weather ahead. As with his now late father before him, this fatal last train ride was also interrupted *en route* at Leipzig by the arrival of his now Imperial Chancellor, Bismarck. On 11 March 1888, he joined his new Imperial masters for the final leg of the journey to Berlin, that was entered amidst a huge snowstorm. Onlookers outside the car saw Bismarck board the new ruler's coach ahead of the other Cabinet ministers, and be kissed on the cheek thrice by the deathly ill monarch, all through the clear window of the curtain-less railroad coach. Thus the new reign officially began. The first Imperial Cabinet meeting then took place in the very same coach. Ominously already having lost his power of speech, His Majesty issued his initial Royal and Imperial commands via writing on a notepad, while his shocked ministers listened in horrified silence as his labored breathing wheezed and gasped via the tubing in his throat. The meeting concluded, the other ministers returned on a separate train to Berlin. Staying behind, Bismarck and his son and aide Herbert received the fatal medical diagnosis from Their Majesties: Frederick III had no more than three-four months of life left to him at most for his reign, and maybe even less if things turned downward.

This Imperial train consisted of a trio of coaches, a sleeper, two saloon cars, and a triad of baggage wagons. It arrived in the Berlin area a little after 11 p.m. that same night, at the West End Station near their new residence, the Charlottenburg Palace. The Imperial entourage was greeted by a crowd from Berlin that had been patiently awaiting the Imperial couple for hours, all in icy winds and banks of heavy snow. Delayed by almost an hour and a half due to the weather, the arrival was described by a local Berlin newspaper:

'We are not leaving here … and we can see the Imperial carriage only in the distance,' one onlooker asserted. 'Our Fritz deserves that we should get our feet cold for him!' said another.

So beloved was he as the Royal who had won a battlefield promotion and a field marshal's baton from his father at Königgrätz 22 years earlier. The people had not forgotten their shining knight. The sick man left the train to enter a sheltering exterior pavilion decorated with palms and flowers, pitched atop rugs within the red-trimmed covering, with embossed golden Prussian eagles, lit by candles.

Also awaiting the new Imperial twosome were all their surviving children and their spouses, who had turned up an hour earlier. Boarding the special train, the Hohenzollern Family rendered a frosty greeting to their parents and Sovereign rulers. Reflecting his long, prior military career, Frederick III appeared clad in cap and long field gray German Army fur-collared overcoat, making his way swiftly out of the tent and through the cold into a closed cab for the journey to his palace.

Thus, 1888 was to become, "The Year of the Three Kaisers" in German history.

Ninety-nine days later—on 15 June 1888—Kaiser Frederick III, 57, "the Idol of the Army," died, and was succeeded by his son, the Crown Prince, Willy, 29, as Kaiser Wilhelm II. His revered grandfather had been Wilhelm I, to whom he always referred as Wilhelm the Great. As one startled observer blurted out in amazement, "Who would have believed it a year ago?" Oddly, there was no coronation.

In 1858, the lifelong happy marriage of Fritz and Vicky had begun with a train ride to Windsor Castle for a brief, two-day honeymoon, after which they left for Germany. Upon their arrival there, they were welcomed at Wittenberg by Field Marshal von Wrangel on behalf of the Army. Inside the carriage with them, the train jolted, and the elderly warlord sat on a large apple tart just given to them. All three laughed uproariously as Princess Vicky had their attendants clean off the field marshal's posterior. The then-Royal couple arrived in Berlin together for the first time as Crown Prince and Princess of Prussia on 8 February 1858.

In 1902—14 years after his death and the year after that of the Empress Frederick—Frederick III's private diaries were published, and in them several of his experiences with trains were noted. During the war of 1866, he recalled:

> I rode with the staff … to a mountain village … close to the Josefstadt-Schwadowitz railway, where I found myself in the center of my army, and could operate in the direction of Nachod or Trautenau, as required … The suburbs of Königgrätz were burning … Not far from a railway at the friendly village of Opatowitz, we were met by a captured gendarme of Benedek's staff [the just defeated Austrian Army commander.] At Pratau … the enemy managed to damage the railway.

Following the war, the Prussian Crown Prince took a private trip to Italy: "We took the train to Bari," and then on to Corfu on 18 October 1869. Egypt was next, via a six-hour railway journey to Cairo. "We reached Cairo at 8 p.m. … The Khedive received us in the Station Buildings … The whole garrison lined the way," from there to, "The landing place of the steamer" ships.

During the war with France, the now Prussian Army commander Fritz noted on 4 August 1870:

> Weissenburg … Gates of the city shot down, and the place taken, thus winning a secure position, and the command of the railways and roads leading to Strasbourg. We had in all two divisions, the enemy one… 5 August: A telegraph book found at the railway station gives important details; i.e., how little prepared the French are with mobilization, formation, and commissariat, and enables one to conjecture that the French Army is concentrating its main force before Metz.
>
> 7 August: During the battle, trains were constantly going to Worth with 60 or more men, who were sent into battle without proper leaders … In (French Marshal) Mac Mahon's (captured) carriage was an accurate map of the Vosges Mountains, along with a plan of all the (rail) connections, which stands us in good stead.…

In 1883, the now Imperial German *Kronprinz* journeyed across Spain to Madrid:

> On the platform, the King was waiting for me in the uniform of our Uhlans.

On 4 December 1883 in Madrid, Fritz noted:

> The King took us today by rail to the *Escorial* (Palace) … which one must have seen in order to appreciate the past glories of Spain … On my

final visit to take leave ... the King then accompanied me to the railway station... I found all the ministers and marshals, the diplomatic corps ... deputations, and country people, and here I ... bade the King 'farewell.'

On 12 December, Frederick decried:

The inadequate heating arrangements of the railway carriages, while the want of variety in the landscape on the long journey to Cordova presented little that was attractive.

At the Sierra Morena:

I involuntarily began to think how easily an accident to the train—which here happens not infrequently, might occur—and what an untoward end such an adventure would make to my journey!

That night, he was awakened from sleep by the arrival at the Alcazar junction of the train of Spanish Queen Isabella:

The conversation ... could have been carried on from window to window, since our carriages were exactly opposite each.... I jumped out ... and paid my respects, in the dead of night, standing on the rails, to the honorable traveler.

During later stops, fruit baskets were handed into the carriage windows by friendly residents, he recalled. Fritz reached Genoa on 16 December, and, "At night embarked on the journey to Rome," by rail again, ending his diary.

On 17 March 1871, the newly-created Field Marshal Crown Prince Frederick—of not only Royal Prussia, but now of Imperial Germany as well—arrived home as the conquering hero of the victorious Franco-Prussian War at Wild Park Station, Potsdam, for a triumphant carriage ride to Berlin. This was just as he and his Imperial father, Kaiser Wilhelm I, had entered surrendered Paris just 16 days earlier.

In 1872, the popular Crown Prince backed a petition in the new German Reichstag for women to:

Be allowed to pursue careers in such professions as the postal, telegraphic, and railway services, bastions of male bureaucracy.

Despite his popularity with the German people, the Crown Prince's liberal governmental views were anathema to both his father and the latter's Imperial Chancellor, Bismarck. Thus, for most of his 17 years as His

Majesty's Imperial Heir, Frederick was given little of real importance to do.

The Crown Prince at 44 in 1877, complained about dashing, "From one (German state) to the other by rail, like a state messenger."

Bleichröder and Bismarck: Banking and Railroading

Gerson von Bleichröder (1822–93) was a German-Jewish banker who made a commercial alliance with Prussian politician von Bismarck. It was during the first railroad economic boom of the 1830s that saw in September 1838 a two-mile-long railway—the Berlin–Potsdam Railroad—extended to Zehlendorf, a trip of under a half hour one way. This was the King of Prussia's own first State Railroad, in which the European Jewish Rothschild banking firm bought shares, and also in other German state railways. By 1850, Prussia as a whole was having its initial general economic boom as well, fueled by these very same railways, financial capital availability, and the growing metallurgy industry. Bleichröder sponsored many new railroad lines, such as the Thuringian railway, being named as well the official banker of both the Cologne–Minden line and also the Rhenish railways. In 1859, then Prussian Prince Regent Wilhelm invited the prominent German-Jewish banker to the opening at Cologne of the Rhine Railroad Bridge he had himself helped fund. It was also during this same prewar period that German railroading first became a virtual cash cow money generator for the next 50 years of both the Prussian and later German state governments. Built during 1833–59, the Cologne-Minden Railroad was the first such, and had been established for the transportation of Ruhr mined coal to Wuppertal, aided by Bleichröder cash. Working in tandem, the "two Bs"— Bismarck and Bleichröder—eventually gained partial but effective Prussian state control over all the country's railway network as well.

The Prussian state suspended its Right of Amortization during 1854–70, a period during which the railroads became German investment's most important sector within the overall economy, with many stocks thereof becoming most profitable, indeed, dominating the German stock markets. Despite this trend, however, four railroads, 61 banks, and 116 industrial firms went bankrupt in 1874, the economic downside of the ending of Bismarck's trio of Unification Wars of 1864–71. With the Reich duly unified at last, Bismarck next set about achieving the same end with all the various German state federal railways as well. Such naturally would eventually entail similar rates, and, hopefully, uniform performance, too. It was expected as well that they would perform better in wartime, known to be necessary after their somewhat disappointing record as shown in the

Gerson von Bleichröder (1822–1893), a German-Jewish banker who made a commercial alliance with Prussian politician Otto von Bismarck.

wars of 1866–71. The economic failures helped Bismarck partially achieve his railway unification aim by 1879, with Bleichröder as his financial handmaiden in acquisitions. Using separate legislative acts of the new *Reichstag/Parliament*, Bismarck proceeded by stages, and by 1890, the Reich duly owned outright 18,683 trackage kilometers, with very few— but still some—private lines left. The Prussian state railways within the German imperium soon became the largest enterprise extant, and were deemed to be reliable, economical, and efficient, protected from disruptive labor strikes as they were by the central government.

The Imperial Chancellor's country estate—Varzin—was but a half-day's train ride from Berlin, and he often resided there for many months of the year, one of the reasons why the later Kaiser Wilhelm II was able to outmaneuver him during 1889–90. It was also during the later stages of the long Bismarckian era that first mention was made of the Berlin-to-Baghdad Railway that became a linchpin project of the subsequent Wilhelmine Age. Banker Bleichröder's overland and seas rail investments included a share in Baron Hirsch's Turkish Railroad network of 1,500,000 Reichsmarks, a first intervention via rail of the Ottoman Empire in the Middle East, fueled in concert with the great Siemens' family German Bank. During 1888–89, German rails and other building materials were sent east in what evolved into Kaiser Wilhelm II's later famed Berlin–Baghdad Railway, or Berlin to Baghdad Railway. The Bismarck–Bleichröder railroads penetrated as well Rumania, with German–Austrian construction being agreed to as well by Bucharest during 1872–89.

Interior view of Prussian Crown Prince's car in 1870, with Kaiser Frederick (center, facing right) being greeted by Prussian Prime Minister von Bismarck at right. At the left of the Kaiser is his wife, Kaiserin Viktoria. They were the parents of Kaiser Wilhelm II. *Library of Congress*

Fritz, Vicky, and Willy

Both His Majesty Kaiser Wilhelm I and Bismarck believed that the root cause of the Crown Prince's liberalism was his wife the *Kronprinzen,* Viktoria, whom neither liked; neither did the anti-British, Prussian-German Army officer corps. All of them doted on the Crown Prince's eldest son Willy—Prince Wilhelm—as a way of splitting him off from his parents. Like the elderly Kaiser and his first Minister, Prince Wilhelm was also a staunch conservative. There was even talk of passing over the Crown Prince in favor of his son when the Old Master died. In his diary entry of 12 September 1874, Prince Wilhelm's tutor and later advisor Georg Hinzpeter recalled:

> We heard the whistle of an engine, and by this knew that at that moment the Emperor was arriving in Kassel in triumph [for the annual autumn military maneuvers], in a comfortable saloon car, honored, extolled, well-dined, in complete enjoyment of a hard-earned position after a lifetime's work; while Prince Wilhelm—having quite insufficiently breakfasted—with tired legs and empty stomach, walked to Kassel, and entered Kassel in the truest manner of a traveling student.

Above left: Nineteen-year-old Wilhelm with his English mother. Wilhelm spoke perfect English and enjoyed having conversations with his grandmother, Victoria, to whom he was very close.

Above right: Crown Princess Victoria (1840–1901), photographed in 1875.

Wilhelm aged 24, some five years before he succeeded his father.

The "Young Master" Takes Over, 1888–90

All of them, however, shared a dark secret—or believed that they did—
and that was that Willy was not mentally fit to rule. In 1877, at age 19, he
and some friends were riding the small switchback railway in the Havel
River's Royal Park on the Pfaueninsel (Isle of Peacocks) of Berlin, when
then Prince Willy playfully scared the other occupants by speeding up
the controls as a lark. This was, in a way, symbolic of the wild up-and-
down, wooly ride of his later 30-year reign of 1888–1918 over the Second
German Reich.

The new Kaiser—Wilhelm II—probably decided long before he became
German Emperor that the old Chancellor would have to go, but on one
thing, at least, they did agree, namely that the German Social Democratic
Party was a grave threat to the Imperial and Royal Thrones. Indeed,
Bismarck told his Imperial Master, "If the Socis strike, then the (future) war
is lost before it starts." In this, the venerable Chancellor was most likely
correct, for almost all of the German railway workers of the Second Reich
were Social Democrats, and a General Strike by them could shut down
the very railroads on which the Army's mobilization plans were entirely
dependent. In August 1914, the Social Democrats supported the Kaiser's
war, however, responding to his appeal to them as fellow Germans only.

Another issue on which they agreed was that Imperial Germany might
find a future ally in Islamic Turkey as, indeed, the Kaiser did in 1914.
Unlike the aging Bismarck's earlier era, during June 1888–March 1890,
Pomeranian grenadiers alone no longer represented younger Germans.
By then, there were also rapacious financiers and train promoters who
saw a glittering future—as did also their young ruler—in the expected
fabulous riches of the Middle East as seen in the Berlin to Baghdad
Railway. To them, the crusty Imperial Chancellor of yesteryear was seen as
an historical figure who represented their past, while in young Willy they
saw their own, joint future greatness of world imperium, global railways,
and powerful naval fleets. In March 1890, the Young Master manipulated
Bismarck's sudden resignation from office, and began thereafter personally
running his governments as he saw fit. Bismarck left the capital of the
empire he had created a generation before on 29 March 1890, seen off
at a Berlin railway station by all the top men of the Reich, but absent the
Kaiser who had fired him. Leaning back in his saloon carriage, Bismarck
archly commented acidly, "A state funeral with full honors!" as the train
glided away to the tunes of a slow march from a martial band. Ironically,
the only prominent Royal who came to see him off was the young Prince
Max of Baden, the Young Master's cousin. In 1918, this same Prince Max
would serve as this Kaiser's last Imperial Chancellor.

After being fired by Kaiser Wilhelm II, Bismarck (right) leaves Berlin's Lehrter Station on 19 March 1890. Note the expressions on everyone's faces. Note also the exterior rail car lamp at left, next to him, and also the overhead partial glass ceiling in the station roof. His main successors were Gen. Count Leo Caprivi (1890–1894), Count Chlodwig von Hohenlohe (1894–1900), Prince Bernhard von Bülow (1900–1909), and Theobald von Bethmann-Hollwegg (1909–1917). *Library of Congress*

Otto von Bismarck late in life.

Late in January 1894, the retired Bismarck returned one last time to Berlin from his country home, being met at the station by His Majesty's younger brother, Prince Heinrich, later a grand admiral in the Kaiser's spanking, brand-new German Imperial High Seas Fleet. This would be a major factor in causing Great Britain to enter the First World War against the Second Reich of Queen Victoria's eldest grandchild—Willy.

When promoted Prince from Count in 1887, Bismarck had been given his own rail car from the Association of German Railways, and a train motif had its place at his death on 30 July 1898. His enemy the young Kaiser, now 40, wanted to exploit his death by an Imperial state funeral in Berlin, but the wily old Chancellor had already foreseen that, and precluded it in his will. He was buried with honors instead in a mausoleum near his retirement home of Friedrichsruh. This tomb was separated from his country mansion by the same railway line that brought the Kaiser and his official mourners to the gravesite, on either side of which stood the opposing factions—family and courtiers—each still embittered at the other, a decade after Bismarck's unceremonious deposition.

German Army Engineer and Railway Troops

By 1900, there were 23 pioneer battalions of 96 companies, plus 17 railroad battalion troops in two and a half regiments, to help manage the growth of Prussian railways of 50 percent that had taken place during 1870–85 and afterwards. During any future railway mobilization, these elite railroad units would help speed it along smoothly it was felt, in face of the enemy, if necessary, according to the 1900 Sigel/von Specht *Report*. This detailed overview noted that all technical railroad fieldwork would be done in wartime by the army's elite pioneer units, with each battalion having sappers, miners, and a pontoon capability. Engineer battalions were also responsible with fortress construction and maintenance, as well as building field redoubts, bridges, railroads, telegraph line and train repairs, and demolition also of same, as necessary. Of its 23 pioneer battalions in the federated German Army of 1871–1918, Prussia boasted 19, Bavaria two, and the Kingdoms of Württemburg and Saxony one each. Oddly, the Engineer command oversaw as well the trio of regiments of the Prussian railway brigade, as well as the sole Royal Bavarian Army railway battalion.

Above: German Army Railway Troops with officer at right and narrow gauge engine at rear, prior to the First World War. Miranda Carter said of Wilhelm II: "Huge sums were spent on the new Imperial train—11 gilded carriages, one big enough to contain a table seating 24." *Library of Congress*

Right: German officer (*left*) and soldier (*right*) standing near railroad tracks, from *The German Army*, 1900. Moltke credited the 1866 Prussian victory over Austria to the railways as well: "We have the ... advantage of being able to carry our field army of 285,000 men ... and virtually concentrating them in five days on the frontiers of Saxony and Bohemia." *Library of Congress*

Engineer officers (*left*) and soldiers in service, undress (*right*), and fatigue (*center*) "uniform," from *The German Army*, 1900. Continued Moltke on 1866: "Austria has only one line of rail, and it will take 45 days to assemble 210,000 men." *Library of Congress*

German Railway Troops at work laying wooden ties and steel rails. *The German Army*

Engineer Soldiers of the 1st and 2nd Railway Regiments and the Engineer Telegraph Company. *The German Army*, 1900. Christian Wolmar said: "At the Battle of Sadowa [1866, the Prussians] beat the Austrians, thanks to the rapid deployment of troops on five available railway lines." *Library of Congress*

The German Military Train

At corps level within the German Army there was a train battalion each of a triad of companies, whose men wore a black leather shako cap and blue uniform with lighter blue shoulder straps depicting the unit number. Each trooper was armed with both carbine and saber. The fully mobilized military train included the battalion staff, a dozen field hospitals, and field telegraph soldiers. The modern German Army had 21 such train battalions, 17 supplied to the Imperial Army by Prussia alone, these consisting of an elite battalion and 16 regular line units. In 1870, these had been led by the well-known Quartermaster-General of the Army, Lt-Gen. Viktor von Podbielski. When in the field, the army's department overseeing its "line of base" consisted of the aforementioned company of pioneers plus both railway and telegraph soldiers, all of whom occasionally performed their combat tasks under enemy fire ahead of even the designated advance guards. It was up to them to establish a trio of main depots, a back-up reserve depot, and 26 branch depots, all of which had to be established as soon as possible once actual operations were underway. By 1900, 60,000 soldiers of all types were being deployed solely to protect these vital lines of base, and were subjected to both rigorous hardships and enemy fire. This was especially true of being vulnerable to the wrath of hostile country

Alfred von Schlieffen (1833–1913) was a German field marshal and strategist who served as Chief of the Imperial German General Staff from 1891 to 1906. His name lived on in the 1905–06 'Schlieffen Plan', a deployment plan and operational guide for a decisive initial offensive operation in a one-front war against the French Third Republic.

peasants and terrorists, the latter ripping up track, tearing down telegraph wires, and delaying Army wagons and stages.

In preparation for the onset of the Great War in 1914, CGS chief Gen. Alfred von Schlieffen wanted a double track railway to serve each German army of 200,000 men. A 50,000-man army group would be assigned 140 trains over a week for a coordinated entrainment. The latter in peacetime entailed annual war game maneuver rehearsals to season both the officers and men to be able to cope with trains blocking lines—as in 1870—as well as damaged or even destroyed bridges in their way. Also as in 1870, special loading and unloading railway platforms were already emplaced, with smaller stations having them also, plus a hard-surfaced road parallel to the tracks to help out in a crisis. The Prussian Army's post-1870 wartime railway regiment consisted of 5,000 officers and enlisted men by 1914, compared to the French 3,000, while the Russian Army was then considering the year 1916 as the target date for when a war with the mighty Second Reich of Wilhelm II would be feasible. It was von Moltke the Younger who made as a precondition for his accepting the post of chief of the General Staff that Kaiser Wilhelm II end his practice of always winning the annual Fall Imperial Military Maneuvers, and His Majesty meekly agreed. No other previous General Staff Chief had ever made such a demand of his All-Powerful Warlord, much less got his way.

Kaiser Bill: Imperial Germany's Traveling Emperor

German diplomat Bernhard von Bülow noted of 1894 in his post-Great War *Memoirs:*

> It was that happy time in Wilhelm II's life when he could indulge his passion for traveling to the full. Berlin humor had christened him the *'Reise-Kaiser' [traveling Emperor],* in contrast to his invalid father the *'leise Kaiser' [quiet Emperor]* and his grandfather, the *'weise Kaiser'* *[wise Emperor].*

In that year of 1894 alone, the Kaiser traveled in the brand-new, famous cream and gold Imperial train nearly 200 days out of 365. Constant motion became a substitute for real work, that he hated. Appearance became reality. Added the Kaiser's own, handpicked memoirist Joachim von Kürenburg:

> This traveling about was largely unnecessary, the reason for it being mostly attendance at reviews, the laying of foundation stones, unveiling of statues, consecration of churches, naming of ships, and swearing in of recruits … The Kaiser's travels involved great expense and a vast amount of trouble. The mere preparations for a journey involved an amount of forethought and planning that few could expect … Apart from the arrangements with the railways, the royal stables, the police, and the wardrobe attendants, all had to receive special orders. The royal uniforms, with their full-dress accessories, cloaks and overcoats; undress uniforms, sabers, swords, sashes, epaulets, helmets, caps, spurs and insignias of orders—*all* had to be selected and packed.… Then there were civilian clothes, shooting costumes, tall hats, yachting and tennis kits, with all their paraphernalia, and there were cases for orders and decorations, caskets for rings and tiepins, tobacco boxes, cigarette cases, watches and silver-or-gold-framed photographs of the Kaiser—to be given as presents on the way. Often the getting ready of all the uniforms and accessories had to be completed within a few hours, for it frequently happened that the route was suddenly changed, making havoc of everything already arranged. The Kaiser's hurried decisions to pack up and start away were the result of his unbridled capriciousness, which earned him the popular and facetious nickname of 'Wilhelm the Sudden.'

Then—just prior to his Imperial departure—His Majesty would issue a stream of directives and telegrams to those he would visit informing them of his imminent arrival on their door steps, including the inevitable

The reception of the Savoyard King Umberto of Italy in Berlin, 1889. His Majesty is seen in black hussar's uniform and busby hat saluting at center right, with a German honor guard at far right standing at present arms with bayonets affixed to their rifles in the station. Kaiser Wilhelm II is at center in white uniform. To the left of the Kaiser is the shorter Italian Crown Prince Vittorio Emanuele, who became king in 1900. He knew both Willy and Hitler, and liked neither. Note also the high, domed ceiling of the railroad station, again, typical architecture of the Wilhelmine Age. *Historical Handke Picture Archives, Library of Congress*

An 1889 Imperial special train arrives somewhere in the Second Reich. His Majesty the Kaiser is seen second from left in white cuirassier's uniform and ornate, eagle-crested helmet, followed by one of his six sons wearing sailor's uniform. Note also the German Railway Service sentries presenting arms at right on the far side of the tracks. The military generally dominated European railways during the Wilhelmine Age. *Library of Congress*

A waiting room furnished for Kaiser Wilhelm II in 1893 at Imperial railway station Potsdam outside Berlin, designed by architect Rundschau. Note the ornate chandeliers. *Library of Congress*

The arrival of Wilhelm II at Koblenz, 1 September 1893.

command to, "Tell the Wild Park Station to have the Royal Train standing ready!" Continued memoirist von Kürenberg:

> When all the many preparations had got so far that the actual start came in sight—always supposing that it was not cancelled at the last minute—the luggage had to be loaded under the supervision of the valet Schulz, who was responsible that nothing was forgotten.

Unlike both his late grandfather and father, their successor demanded a fabulous new Imperial Train befitting the expected grandeur of his coming New Course era and reign. What emerged was an Imperial cream-and-gold train of a dozen carriages, with a saloon car upholstered in vibrant blue satin.

Not for the grandson of Kaiser Wilhelm I was the aged former monarch's former custom of eating *en route* in either a hot or cold, tiny railroad station dining room. Instead, he ate in the splendid dark blue and ivory conveyance outside, featuring white and gold interiors. He had his very own personal, plush dining car, as well as the newest saloon coach lit by an overhead chandelier, and also a luxurious bathing carriage. In addition, there were coaches for the large Imperial entourage, a cook's car, and space as well for an extensive wardrobe of all the various uniforms with the trappings so beloved of Wilhelm II that he would sport *en route*, all contained in their own luggage vans. A pair of locomotives were always on hand with steam up to provide the excessive speed so treasured by the vain monarch. Indeed, while negotiating dangerous curves, his staff had to put up with having the contents of their plates and bowls being splashed over them. Sleeping, too, was also better at reduced speeds, but here as well, Kaiser Bill relished roaring through the countryside even in the dead of night.

Surprisingly, Prussian state railway regulations required even His Majesty to pay mileage on his rail trips, but once in foreign lands, his trains usually traveled for free, courtesy of the host governments. The new ruler scandalized his grief-stricken mother that very June of 1888 at his accession by leaving Berlin in mourning for his father to make his first official visit as German Sovereign to Tsar Alexander III of Russia, who disliked him. His Majesty was generally off a-training for all of that first summer, and into the fall of 1888. The new Kaiser was also very keen on training to his favorite Imperial Hunting Lodge on Rominten's moors in East Prussia, disembarking at its small country station. Nor was that first restless spring-fall the zenith of His Majesty's restless rail jaunts, but, rather, only the start, increasing in number, complexity, and cost every month for almost all 30 years of his long reign. The railhead at St

The Earl of Lonsdale with the Kaiser's adjutants and aides de camp during the manoeuvres of 1905.

Kaiser Wilhelm II—again in civilian garb, second from left— arrives by rail at Bari on a Wagonlits car, 1905. He once joked with Franz Ferdinand, "Don't think that I've come to welcome you! I'm here for the arrival of the Crown Prince of Italy!" *Library of Congress*

Wearing civilian suit, the Kaiser (left) arrives for a visit to England in 1907, during the reign of his uncle, King Edward VII. *Library of Congress*

King Edward VII visiting his nephew Kaiser Wilhelm II at Friedrichshof during the state visit of 1909. Three of Kaiser's four sisters are at left.

Above and Below: Interior views of Kaiser Wilhelm II's imperial train salon car on display at Berlin in 1935.

Petersburg was followed in quick succession by Stockholm, Copenhagen, Vienna, and Rome, and off to the German seacoast for crossing over the English Channel to the United Kingdom. These gadabouts included the train's being equipped with a listed, "80 diamond rings, 150 silver orders, 50 breastpins, three gold photograph frames, 30 gold watches and chains, 100 caskets, and 20 diamond-set Orders of the Black Eagle," noted one rendering. Indeed, reportedly, the Imperial anthem had become—so asserted Berlin wags—*Heil dir in Sonderzug [Hail to Thee in Special Train]*… The Imperial anthem really began with, *Heil dir in Siegerkranz [Hail to Thee in conqueror's crown.]*

His famous dining car table sat 24, while five sleeping cars accommodated gentlemen travelers with His Majesty, as well as their ladies and servants all. There were also a brace of guest saloon cars furnished with sofas, writing desks, and plush armchairs. Occasionally, the Kaiser was joined on board the train by his revered Empress and Consort, Kaiserin Augusta Viktoria of Schleswig-Holstein, nicknamed Dona. During 1894 alone—in the sixth year of the reign—the Berlin press estimated that the Kaiser spent 199 days aboard his train out of only the past 12 months. It was joked about on Berlin streets that his lament was, "I have no time to *rule!*" After Queen Victoria died suddenly in 1901, he reportedly got the ride of his life on the British railway system on the personal train of the new English King, Edward VII detested being late. The King's engineer was told to make up for lost time by increasing speed, and when 90 mph was reached past Holmwood on the infamous reverse curve near Dorking, many passengers aboard who knew of them in advance feared that the Royal Train would be derailed—and all to gain but nine lost minutes! There was even a posted speed limit of 20 mph at the embankment's foot, and all were truly anxious as a result. A fatal accident might have altered much in European history. Even the old Queen—who disliked speed and the London, Brighton, and South Coast Railway, allegedly—kept her last appointment with two minutes in hand. As for the excited Kaiser—used as he had become to the rocking of his own Royal Train—he dispatched an adjutant to tell the British driver that he was astonished that, "So small an engine could go so fast!"

Above and Below: Four interior views of Kaiser Wilhelm II's imperial train including Kaiserin Augusta Viktoria's parlor car interior view, 1910 and her sleeping car. *Library of Congress*

Kaiserin Augusta
Viktoria of
Schleswig-Holstein
(1858–1921) in a 1913
portrait photograph.

Kaiser Wilhelm II in bicorn hat at left leaving his Imperial train with an honor guard
with rifles and bayonets facing him at left also. *Library of Congress*

Prussian royal train of the King of Prussia and German Kaiser in 1910. *Library of Congress*

The Royal Prussian train stationed in the main Potsdam workshops outside Berlin. Bülow wrote in 1931: "When the Kaiser was on his way back to the railway station from the Bremen City Hall … a workman threw a piece of iron at the Imperial carriage. The Kaiser received a considerable wound on the right cheek. He might easily have lost his right eye. Bleeding profusely, the Kaiser arrived at Bremen Station, having retained complete self-control … When I called for him … at the Lehrter Station he showed no excitement whatsoever, and he mentioned the incident only with amiable equanimity … His attitude was really beyond all praise. It was truly regal." *Library of Congress*

An Imperial special train baggage car in 1910. Notes Rohl: His Majesty, "As 'supreme head' of the Reich Railways and postal services" could monitor and direct, "The architecture of stations and post offices as he saw fit," and did, too. *Library of Congress*

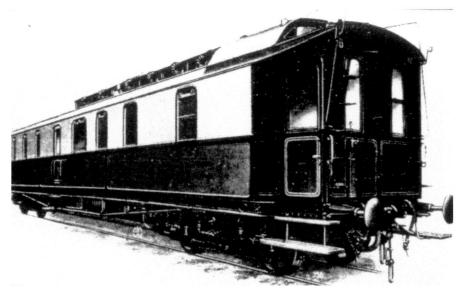

Above and below: More views of the Kaiser's imperial special train personal car displayed in the exhibition hall at Berlin in 1935, during Hitler's Third Reich. *Library of Congress*

German Imperial Chancellor Prince Bernhard von Bülow on Railways

Most top officials in the know worried about the Kaiser's restless mental state as reflected in, "The chasing from place to place," as Imperial Chancellor Prince Bernhard von Bülow once so aptly put it. "I foresee … the finish … of Wilhelm II." The officials of the high Wilhelmine Age were railway travel snobs, as he also noted in his postwar memoirs:

> In these modern days, 'gentlemen' might be placed in the awful position of having to share a second-class and even a first-class compartment with people who wore detachable cuffs!

Of the famous Tsarist Russian premier and career railroader Sergei Witte, von Bülow observed, "He had special knowledge of the railway system." Of German official Dr Karl Helfferich, he also noted, "A railway disaster was to put a sudden and tragic end to the schemes and aspirations of this gifted man."

When the famed British colonialist Cecil Rhodes visited Berlin on 11 March 1899, he and the Kaiser discussed, "The broad outlines of his project of an all-British Cape-to-Cairo railway. The Kaiser's eyes shone. Britain's Boer War—in which a young Winston Churchill made a spectacular escape from captivity by train—was very unpopular in the Second Reich, and when King Edward VII came to Germany in February 1901 to visit his dying elder sister the Empress Frederick, Bülow stated, "The public assembled at the railway stations" along his route to demonstrate their anger. Later, he wrote that:

> I realized that German unity had been more effectively promoted by our system of transportation than by anything else. Railways and telegraphs were the greatest enemies of all particularism. If one could travel comfortably from the Baden to the Hessian capital in two hours, no serious differences between these two States were really possible.

Bernhard Heinrich Karl Martin von Bülow
(1849–1929). Von Bülow served as Secretary of
State for Foreign Affairs for three years and then
as Chancellor of the German Empire from 1900
to 1909.

The mighty Krupp works at Essen, 1890. Krupp provided much of the steel required
for the Reich.

The Kaiser's Grandiose Dream:
The Berlin to Baghdad Railway via Turkey, Syria, & Iraq

From the very first days after his 15 June 1888 accession to the Throne, young Willy wanted to enact a grand political and military alliance with the Turks in the Middle East. His initial trip to Constantinople took place in 1889, with the Middle East balance of power put at odds. The Kaiser's railroad representatives signed the initial Berlin to Baghdad Railway concessions that allowed the Second Reich to build its first Middle Eastern line into present-day Iraq. This was not surveyed, however, until a year later, in 1900, the year after His Majesty's second state visit to Turkey. The Turkish capital's resident German foreign office resident personally surveyed the proposed new overland route in the company of a large group. Even though this projected line was to end at Baghdad, the Germans pressed on, to the Persian Gulf oil sheikdom of Kuwait, where the new Baghdad Railway Company wanted land to erect a shipping port on the Kuwaiti Gulf. Not too surprisingly, though, Turkey's ancient foes the Kuwaitis rejected outright this unofficial request of Kaiser Billy's.

Nonetheless, both the Kaiser and his main Turkish ally—the ruling Sultan Abdul Hamid II—pressed on with their joint ambitious railway scheme. The Turkish ruler was greedy for the cash from a Western ruler he then believed had no territorial interests in his own lands. In 1899, he signed off on the projected railroad that remained the property of the Ottoman Empire via treaty. The two monarchs then dually funded it via their governments east and west with both loans and operational contracts. Over time, the Sultan and his subsequent non-Royal Ottoman rulers feared that the German financial loans would lead to Imperial Turkish bankruptcy, thus allowing the *Kaiserreich* to simply seize the new railroad in default of any loan repayment.

Meanwhile on the construction sites tough labor conditions caused illness combined with the tediousness of round-the-clock tunneling. On the cusp of war in 1914 the Berlin to Baghdad Railway was nowhere near completion. The war in the Near and Middle East began well in the summer and fall of 1914, with the Turks still holding their own ground, and not, therefore, under Germanic sway. By 1915, however, the Berlin to Baghdad Railway had financial problems caused by the war and a lack of supplies not alleviated enough via the deployment of captured British prisoners-of-war working on the construction site. The entire project was overtaken by the British Army's seizure of Baghdad itself in 1917. Thus, the Berlin to Baghdad Railway never had any real strategic impact to the Central Powers versus the Allies, either prewar or in wartime. Simply put, the war handicapped railroad building, while incomplete sections

Sultan Abdul Hamid II (1842–1918) in a carriage with Kaiser Wilhelm II. Abdul Hamid was the 34th Sultan of the Ottoman Empire and the last Sultan to exert effective autocratic control over Turkey.

Digging into a hillside on the Berlin to Baghdad Railway construction, 1905.

likewise hampered the overall war effort in the region: a vicious circle never broken. It did, however, safeguard Turkish Anatolia; it also spurred economic growth and later helped Turkey's First World War hero of Gallipoli, Kemal Ataturk.

The mere concept of its sweeping vistas prewar excited railway promoters in both Berlin and Vienna, and conversely alarmed those in London, Paris, and St Petersburg. The railway was just part of what had had worried the later wartime Allies prior to the war. By 1913, Imperial Germany's population was 66 million people out of 460 million in Europe overall. In steel production for 1910, Germany accounted for half that of the much larger United States, more than double that of Great Britain, more than four times that of Republican France, and more than six times that of Imperial Russia.

Dr Karl Helfferich was appointed Assistant General Manager of the Anatolian Railway in 1906 at the age of 34, the son-in-law of Dr

Karl Theodor Helfferich (1872–1924) was a politician, economist, and financier. In 1902 Helfferich entered upon a diplomatic career and soon became a leader in the German government's policy of economic imperialism, and in 1906 he was appointed director of the Anatolian Railway which was financed by Deutsche Bank. He was Secretary for the Treasury from 1916 to 1917, and was said to be responsible for financing expenses for the First World War through loans instead of taxes. He counted upon a final German victory and upon imposing heavy indemnities upon the Allies. *Library of Congress*

Siemens—then head of the German Bank—that was behind the Berlin to Baghdad Railway. Dr Helfferich later became director of the bank, and was Germany's finance minister during part of the First World War. In 1912, the Second Reich had a 220 per cent increase in its total import–export trade in millions of marks, versus but 100 percent for that of the United Kingdom, 170 percent for the U.S., and 100 percent for France. The first phase of the Berlin to Baghdad Railway during 1888–99 was as a commercial venture, but as long ago as 1835, Moltke the Elder had foreseen the martial value of just such a line when he had served as Prussian military advisor to the Turks.

An initial much shorter railway had been built first, in 1871, with Wilhelm von Pressel's engineering surveys impressing the Sultan at Istanbul. It was not until 1888, though, that Dr Siemens had been able to launch an actual paper entity known as the Anatolian Railway Company that took over an existing British line to push it forward to South Anatolia. When Bismarck opposed it, Wilhelm II vetoed his Imperial Chancellor and proceeded. It evolved as a quiet, commercial venture, with the Germans directing their railways competently and honestly, the Turks being suitably impressed. During 1899–1908, there occurred the second phase drive to the east. In 1897, a Greco-Turkish war had been won in which German railways had a significant part, and it was this military factor that prompted the Sultan to favor an expansion of the Berlin to Baghdad Railway, politically aided by the Kaiser's second state visit in 1899. It was concluded on 27 November 1899 with the Kaiser being paid for each kilometer of track lain as an incentive, known as the Kilometer Guarantees. Additional pro-German train provisions covered the establishment of irrigation works for arid land, harbors, and related industries on the rail right of way. The Sultan authorized state revenues being paid out via specified revenues earmarked in advance for the railway. Projected routes ran from Haidar Pasha on the Asiatic side of Istanbul on through Ankara, Adana, Mosul, Aleppo, Baghdad, Basra, and the Persian Gulf. Both the Russians and the British presented repeated diplomatic objections asserting that the contested railroad violated their own regional interests.

Turkey gained numerous benefits: it was better than other European projected railways, connected Turkey's far-flung Imperial provinces, and traveled through Anatolia's Taurus Mountains, as opposed to along the coast from Alexandretta to Aleppo, thus freeing it from being attacked by any future naval warfare there. Finally— rightly or wrongly— the Turks felt that the Germans would not try to annex any lands that the railway serviced. An editorial in *The Times* of London stated on 30 November 1889 that, "There is no Power into whose hands Englishmen would more gladly see the enterprise fall than Germany's." What was probably meant, however, was "and not Russia's."

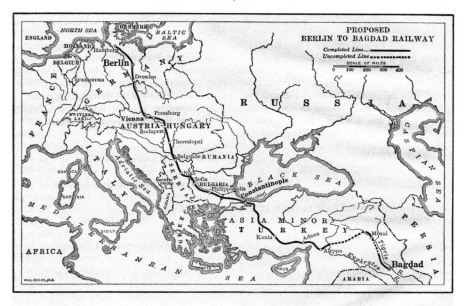

An early map of the Berlin to Baghdad Railway.

An engine and wagons on the Berlin to Baghdad Railway. *Library of Congress*

The opening years of 1899–1902 were rather fallow overall, with a "final" grant announced on 18 March 1902 to the government of von Bülow. When he asked for both British and French private loans, the British press raised loud objections. Diplomatically, Whitehall privately asked Istanbul to cool down the railway's forward thrust, and also to delay tariff increases to fund the construction. In the 1908–13 third phase concessionary, the Germans agreed to turn over to Turkey the Baghdad–Basra extension. Moreover, in 1910 at Potsdam, a Russian zone of influence in Persia was conceded by Berlin, and in February 1914, France, too, received one, in Syria and Northern Anatolia. This led to successful negotiations between the German Bank and the French-influenced Ottoman Bank, from which the German sphere and its Anatolian Railway was recognized a mere six months prior to the Great War. Ultimately, the Kaiser wanted the Berlin to Baghdad Railway to connect with his colony in German East Africa, but war prevented this. Despite wartime disruption and subsequent depression and upheaval the Berlin to Baghdad Railway was finally completed in 1940.

On 5 June 1914, Britain, too, signed on in a way that seemed to foreshadow some future German–UK–Turkish cooperation. Among the terms was the recognition of German railroad hegemony in most Turkish areas and an Adana monopoly; the Basra extension being halted; British control to its south, Turkish customs money to increase, British monopoly in Mesopotamia, and established as an open body of water the Shatt-al-Arab also. One observer noted: "There is no doubt that Britain got the best of this arrangement." She had halted the railroad building, thus hampering future wartime Turkish Army troop deployment. A 1903 German article written by Dr Paul von Rohrbach in the periodical *The Baghdad Railway* asserted that:

England can be attacked in only one place: Egypt... Turkey, however, can never dream of recovering Egypt [lost in 1882] until she is mistress of a developed railway system through Asia Minor and Syria, and until—through the progress of the Anatolian Railway to Baghdad—she is in a position to withstand an attack by England upon Mesopotamia. The policy of protecting Turkey—that is now pursued by Germany—has no other object but the desire to affect an insurance against the danger of a war with England.

Another observer believed that the Berlin to Baghdad Railway "was at most" a minor irritant between England and Germany up to 1914 and the war. The first train from Berlin to Constantinople was on 17 January 1916, at the very height of the First World War. American Ambassador to Turkey Henry Morgenthau (1913–16) later recalled that:

There was great rejoicing in Constantinople ... The railroad station was decorated with flags and flowers, and the whole German and Austrian population—including the embassies' staffs—turned out to welcome the incoming train ...

Northwest to southeast, the Berlin to Baghdad Railway from Konya–Basra connected Anatolia, Eregli, the Taurus Mountains, Gulek Pass, the Cukurova Plain, Yenice, Adana, the Amanus Range, Aleppo, Nuisaybin, Mosul, Baghdad, and Basru, with much of the building being done by Philip Holzmann. Britain feared a Berlin–Baghdad proximity to its Persian oilfields that supplied the Royal Navy with much of its oil supplies.

1908 German Field Service Lines of Communication Regulations Report

These stated partially that:

A railway station—to serve as a home base—will be assigned to every army corps. From these home bases, supplies are sent forward to collecting depots ... that will be established at not too great a distance from the theater of war ... A base will be assigned to each army ... according to the progress of the operations. The army corps are connected with the field base by lines of communication roads, and on

A train on the Pekdemir viaduct on a completed section of the Berlin to Baghdad Railway, *c.* 1910.

these roads, posts are formed about 13½ miles apart. As for the mass of working details also included in the various regulations, these may well appear to provide in advance for every possible requirement of entire armies, down to the supply of drinking water at stations, and the taking of carrier pigeons in the troop trains.

Mighty Imperial Germany, 1914

The Second Reich's comprehensive railway expansion was founded on her massive coal, steel, and iron central growth, with the booming railway network infrastructure propelling it. Indeed, during 1870–1913, total Reich railroad trackage *doubled* in kilometers to the year before the Great War. The Berlin to Baghdad Railway mania had been sparked in 1896 with the planned line of Berlin–Konia in the Turkish Anatolian Mountains of a thousand new kilometers of new rails to be built in less than eight years in a deprived economic area. A real engineering and building achievement by 1902 in Mesopotamia, this rich Ottoman Imperial province boasted what was termed as, "A veritable lake of oil."

The French-sponsored Trans-Sahara Railway project was designed to link the interior of Africa from Dakar in French Senegal in West Africa to French Djibouti on the Red Sea in East Africa, across the waist of the Dark

The arrival of Kaiser Wilhelm II (center, wearing Reich Hunt uniform) at Konopišt⊠, Bohemia, two weeks before the murder by a Serbian assassin at Sarajevo, Serbia on 28 June 1914 of the man at the far left wearing Prussian Uhlan uniform and helmet, Austrian Grand Duke and Heir to the Throne, Franz Ferdinand. His murder and that of his wife also—Sophie Chotek—helped spark the First World War that saw both their monarchies overthrown four years later. *Historical Handke Picture Archives, Library of Congress*

Rhine Riverbank parlor car of the German Crown Prince Wilhelm (second from left, being saluted by a railway official.) The woman in white at center is Crown Princess Cecilie, both being here greeted upon an official pre-Great War event. *Library of Congress*

How it all started. Gavrilo Princip (1894–1918) is arrested following his assassination of Archduke Franz Ferdinand of Austria and his wife, Sophie, Duchess of Hohenberg, in Sarajevo on 28 June 1914. Princip and his accomplices were arrested and implicated several members of the Serbian military, leading Austria-Hungary to issue a démarche to Serbia known as the July Ultimatum. This was used as pretext for Austria-Hungary's invasion of Serbia, which then led to the First World War.

Continent. Meanwhile, the Russians were building their own vast, Trans-Siberian Railway, a mammoth 5,400-mile long line. The Kaiser referred in a letter to the Berlin to Baghdad Railway as, "My railroad. I created it, and it remains my work!" As early as 1882, however, his mother the Crown Princess Frederick had asserted that it would be disastrous should

> The Germans instead of the English make the Euphrates Valley railway … We English have an interest in the east, and not the French and Germans!

By 1899, her son Willy as Kaiser was having none of this, relating his meeting with Englishman Cecil Rhodes, who told him that he (the Kaiser) should, "Build the railway through Asia Minor to the Euphrates—the land route to India." Certainly, he added, His Majesty had not gone to Jerusalem just to see the holy places, but, rather, had "other aims" there. The Kaiser, ecstatic at this, chortled, "You have guessed right! I shall build this railway, and reopen these lands of ancient civilization to the world!"

3

The Great War, 1914–18

Pvt. A. Hitler's 1914 Troop Train

Like most of the new enlistees in August 1914 in the German Army's 16th Bavarian Infantry (List) Regiment, Pvt. Adolf Hitler, 25, thought that victory over the Allies would be Germany's by New Year's Day, 1915. Ten years later, writing in *Mein Kampf/My Battle* he recalled:

> For the first time, I saw the Rhine as we rode westward along its quiet waters to defend it. The old *Watch on the Rhine* roared out of the endless transport train into the morning sky, and I felt as though my heart would burst.

Kaiser Bill Also Heads West

The Kaiser's Naval Cabinet Chief—Vice Adm. Georg von Müller—wrote in his diary for 6 July 1914:

> We left Wild Park Station [at Potsdam] at 9:15. Uninterrupted conversation in the dining car all the way to Kiel. His Majesty … received representatives of the War Minister, General Staff, Admiralty Staff, and Reich Navy Office to discuss the situation which would arise from the planned invasion by the Austrians of Serbia.

The Kaiser hurried off to the Western Front secure in the knowledge that he had behind—or under—him the most extensive military rail network on the entire European Continent.

Jubilant German Army troops on their way to Paris by rail, August 1914; they never made it during the war, however. Note also the cartoon of French Gen. Joseph "Papa" Joffre being chalked on the side of the car at center. *Library of Congress*

His Majesty the King of Prussia and German Kaiser Wilhelm II at center, holding informal swagger stick Field Marshal's baton with crowned hilt in his damaged left hand, with his staff leaving the imperial train on a wartime front inspection tour. Note also the Red Cross man at right and the Imperial Standard Bearer at center, *Library of Congress*

Mobilization!

Off to war! Enthusiastic conscripts on their way to the west.

The enthusiasm in Germany was profound and initially the concept of the war was popular. No-one gave a thought to how it might turn out.

The German Railway System in 1914

The Norton *Report* of 1905 had compared the then rival commercial passenger railways of the UK and the Reich:

> In Great Britain, it requires years of travel and careful observation to learn one's way across the country and its numerous lines, and to avoid the many pitfalls which are everywhere placed in the way of the inexperienced traveler. In Germany, such pitfalls do not exist, and the greatest simpleton will travel as cheaply, comfortably, and rapidly all over the country as will the most cunning commercial traveler. In Germany, railway trains arrive— in 19 times out of 20—to the minute, because the government punishes severely those who are responsible for delay. The German freight tariff is of beautiful simplicity … Every trader possesses a little book by means of which the office boy can calculate in a moment the exact amount of the freight charges for any weight between two stations.

In 1913, the Reich was generally conceded to have Europe's biggest and most powerful locomotive engines by far, but they were also smaller than the-then most modern North American standard version. Tunnel clearances and bridge capacities were then restricted to trains up to 120 axles, or 30 cars, with a top load capacity of 15 tons apiece. Certain engines were posted to particular engineer-and-foreman teams, with higher power given to double-crews for daily working maintenance. Fires were stoked up two hours prior to leave time, while this same early preparation also allowed for the crew to hostle the engine. By contrast, the engineers reported an hour prior to leaving, while the engine crew took care of all other, related departure details. At tour's end, crews remained for any final engine adjustments, and then concluded their shift. Company policy mandated that all crews have eight hours off in between shifts, for safety's sake and necessary rest. Fuel efficiency running improvements recorded resulted in company-awarded bonuses. Better fuel bricks meantime were produced from the Reich's domestic lower-quality brown coal, used when less smoke or an added evaporative level was necessary. One amused onlooker noted that: "With the assigned engines, the men act as if they were footing the fuel bills themselves!" Reportedly, the Reich Railways paid its men lower wages than their opposite numbers in the United States, but in higher contrast, the German railway men also received subsidized housing for the crews and their families close to the city rail terminals at which they worked. Train management officials likewise lived in cut-rate apartments within their own terminal buildings. This followed the same pattern established in most period Western industrial countries of paid for "company towns" that also served to contain the entire railway work force in sustained and compact locations, permanently. This also meant that the same work force was also on call 24 hours daily. This was true in both cases mainly because all living quarters were on state property. Children generally followed their parents into railroading careers across several succeeding generations. As noted by one railway expert:

> Failing to stay on schedule was a serious transgression in peacetime. With a loyal, cohesive group of railroaders conditioned to follow standardized procedures … one can imagine that German troop and supply trains would run like clockwork …

As war threatened, Col. Erich Ludendorff was chief of the German Army's Deployment Section, while Capt. Wilhelm Groener was in the railway Section. In March 1914, there were discussions in Berlin as to how best to entrain the Italian Army for transit over the Alps. At that time, Savoyard Italy was a member of the Triple Alliance with Imperial

Karl Eduard Wilhelm Groener (1867–1939) was a soldier and politician. His organisational and logistical abilities resulted in a successful military career before and during the First World War.

Germany and Austria-Hungary, but when war broke out in August, she declared her neutrality. After the First Battle of the Marne was lost by the Germans, Italy began secret negotiations with the Allies that led to her declaration of war against Austria in May 1915.

The German Imperial Railway Administration of *Elsass-Lothringen*

Territory contested for centuries between Metropolitan France and "Germany" has been known to the French as Alsace-Lorraine, and to the Germans as Elsass-Lothringen. In 1871, the newly declared German Second Reich annexed already occupied Alsace-Lorraine as a province or semi-independent *Reichsland* of the German Empire created by Bismarck. It was then administered by Imperial governors appointed by the new Kaisers, who held sway over both the civil ministry and legislature. The French took it back in 1919. The local German Elsass-Lothringen railway administration was also based at Strasbourg, along with the civil and military regimes. As a result of the German Treaty of Frankfurt that concluded the Franco-Prussian War, the Alsace-Lorraine French railways of the Company of Chemins of the East were duly Germanized, with Aryan officials, station nomenclature, and even rolling stock. This was followed by a rapid ramp-up expansion of the entire combined system, in preparation for the next war.

By 1918, the total length of the E-L railway had been tripled in size by a modern, dense train network grid, as the transit system of the Reich's industrial locus, and of Central Europe. In addition to being wealthy in natural resources, the region formed a geographical linkage among France, Germany, Luxembourg, Switzerland and—via the German Rhineland—Belgium and The Netherlands. Capitalizing on this geographical feature, the Reich railways considered E-L to be the very "hinge" in its overall Central European railway network. This latter connected both the German North Sea outlet via Belgium and Holland to France over a pass in the rugged French Vosges Mountains. The DRG's Imperial railway administration coordinated as well with Royalist Savoyard Italy in the building of the celebrated St Gotthard Tunnel, a Swiss–German style counterpart to the French–Italian Mt. Cenis Pass, in a true international railway grid spirit.

Kaiser Wilhelm II: "The Man of Peace"—The Norton *Report*

In the summer of 1914, the American Roy Norton (1870–*c*.1942) compiled a series of *Reports* issued during 1914–15 designed to justify Great Britain's decision to enter the Great War on the Allied side of Russia and France against Imperial Germany and Austria-Hungary. In his view, the "Man of Peace"—Kaiser Wilhelm II—was to blame for the start of the war, and the one who stated, "Our military railways are now perfected." Norton reported:

> I did observe that … scattered over Germany were more of those wonderful 'switch' or 'shunting' yards, capable of entraining tens of thousands of soldiers in a few hours…when from 10–20 passenger trains could be drawn up at one time, and … some of these queer yards—all equipped with electric lighting plants—are out in places where there are not a dozen houses in sight. In some of these yards—located at central points for rural mobilization—one saw long trains of troop cars: dingy, empty, stodgily waiting for use in war, if one ever came. I was told of one test mobilization (in reply to my query as to why I had seen so many troops pass through a small space one evening), where 20,000 men were assembled at 10 a.m., made a camp complete, were reviewed, entrained, detrained, and just seven hours later, there was nothing save debris and trampled grass to show that the place had ever been disturbed. At a mere 'tank station' (i.e., the location of a water tank to replenish locomotive tenders with no civilian settlement) below Kriesingen on 12 June 1914, I saw probably

75-100 locomotives, most of which were of an antiquated type obsolete as far as the demands of up-to-date traffic are concerned, and of a kind that would have been 'scrapped' in either England or America, yet these were being cared for and 'doctored up.' A few engineers and stokers worked round them, and I saw them run one down a long track and bring it back to another, whereupon hostlers at once began drawing its fires, and the engineer and stoker crossed over and climbed into another cab. 'What do you suppose they are doing that for?' I asked one of the trainmen with whom I struck up an acquaintance. 'Why,' he replied with perfect frankness, 'those are war locomotives.' Reading the look of bewilderment on my face, he added, 'You see, those engines are no longer good enough for heavy or fast traffic, so as soon as they become obsolete, we send them to the reserve…all of them are good enough to move troop trains, and therefore are never destroyed. They are all frequently fired up and tested in regular turn. Those fellows out there do nothing else. That is their business, just keeping those engines in order and fit for troop duty. There are dozens of such depots over Germany.' 'But how on earth could you man them in case of war? Where would you get the engineers for so many extras?'

He smiled pityingly at my ignorance. 'The headquarters know to the ton what each one of these can pull, how fast, where the troops are that it will pull, and every man who would ride behind one has the number of the car he would ride in, and for every so many men, there is waiting somewhere a reserve engineer and stoker. The best locomotives would be the first out of the reserve, and so on down to the ones that can barely do 15 kilometers per hour.' Since that June day, Germany has proved how faithfully those thousands of reserve locomotives over her domain have been nursed and cared for, and how quickly those who were to man and ride behind them could respond … On 14 February of this year, I was in Cologne, and blundered … into what I learned was a military stores yard…. There were tiny locomotives loaded on flats which could be run off those cars by an ingenious contrivance of metal … rails. Also, there were other flats loaded with sections of tracks fastened on cup ties (sleepers that can be laid on the surface of the earth), and sections of miniature bridges on other flats. I saw how it was possible to lay a line of temporary railway, including bridges, almost anywhere in an incredibly short space of time, if one had the men. At one period of my life, I was actively interested in railway construction, but had never before seen anything like this! I discovered that I was on forbidden ground, and had to leave, but the official who directed me out told me that what I had seen were construction outfits … I was puzzled by the absence of dump cars, and that mass of smaller paraphernalia to which I had been accustomed in all the contracting work I had ever seen. I had to remember in admiration the ingenuity of the outfit, and think of how quickly it could all be laid, transferred, re-shipped, or stored.

He recalled the letter he received from a Hollander that reached Norton at home on 30 August 1914, after war had been declared:

> Never, I believe, did a country so thoroughly get ready for war! I saw the oddest spectacle, the building of a railway behind a battlefield. They had diminutive little engines and rails in sections, so they could be bolted together, and even bridges that could be put across ravines in a twinkling: flat cars that could be carried by hand and dropped on the rails, great strings of them. Up to the nearest point of battle came—on the regular railway— this small one. At the point where we were, it came up against the soldiers. It seemed to me that hundreds of men had been trained for this task, for, in but a few minutes, that small portable train was buzzing backward and forward on its own, small portable rails, distributing food and supplies. It was a great work, I can tell you! In battle, it would be possible for those sturdy little trains [narrow gauge trains] to shift troops to critical or endangered points at the rate of perhaps 20 mph, keep ammunition, batteries, etc., moving at the same rate, and, of course, be of inestimable use in clearing off the wounded. A portable railway for a battlefield struck me as coming about as close to making war by machinery as anything I have ever heard of. I did not have a chance, however, to see it working under fire, for—being practically a prisoner—I was hurried onward, and away from the scene.

Norton concluded his 1915 *Report*:

> I know of nothing more than this—coming from one whom I know to be truthful—that so adequately shows how even ingenious details had been worked out for military perfection. We shall… hear, after this war is over, how well those field trains performed their work when it came to shifting troops in times of fierce pressure on a threatened point, and how it added to German efficacy.

War by Railway Timetables: How Railroads Started the First World War

By 1914, the "critical distance" factor necessary for wartime trains to be considered effective had fallen to 50 miles, down by half since 1860. In planning for his maximum railway war versus France, Moltke the Younger did so based on the false assumption that Russia would not be ready for war herself until 1916, and by then, he reasoned, Republican France would be vanquished again, just as she had been in 1871, this mistaken notion having been "confirmed" by German spies. Therefore, on 1 June 1914, Moltke asserted, "We are ready, and the sooner the better for us!" As the political as well as the military leader of the nation, Wilhelm II was not so sure. The All-Powerful Warlord recalled that even Frederick the Great had lost his own capital of Berlin to the Russian Army of his era during the very nearly lost Seven Years' War of 1757–63. It could happen again, he reasoned.

"The Other Side of the Hill:" Russia in 1914

Unknown to the cocky and despised Prussians, Tsar Nicholas II (1868–1918) in 1912 had earmarked fully 800,000 troops of the Imperial Russian Army for his own planned drive on the hated Kaiser's Berlin. This was despite the fact that none of His Majesty's railways were up to such a military operation over long distances, and also—once on German territory of invaded East Prussia—his trains would be faced with the enemy's different gauge. Nevertheless—and completely dumbfounding the Kaiser's top military geniuses at Berlin—it was the allegedly "unprepared" Russian Army that invaded Germany in summer 1914. Because there was no east–west railway across Russian Poland into East Prussia, though, the Russian 2nd Army of Gen. Alexander Samsonov crossed the Russo-German frontier two days behind that of Gen. Pavel Rennenkampf's 1st Army. On 17 August 1914, the latter's two cavalry corps were effectively cutting both branches of the enemy railway to halt the escape of German rolling stock, as well as screening his own victorious advance further into East Prussia. It was then, though that the deliberate usage of different Russian gauge to stymie an always expected German Army invasion of Mother Russia came to halt the Russians in the Second Reich. The Russian Army was totally unable to use its captured DRG rails without captured German trains, most of which their enemy spirited away as fast as it could. Nor did the Russians deploy its own rolling stock on the captured DRG lines for the very same reason. Accordingly, the Russian Army almost immediately outran its Eighteenth Century horse-drawn supply carts. Their communications situation was just as tenuous, with the Tsar's army forced to rely on German telegraph lines and even offices, as it lacked its own wire-laying capacity. As the Russians came upon these offices already destroyed by the retreating Germans, they simply sent their own messages over whatever wires were taken intact in the clear, as their divisional staffs were also bereft of both military codes and the cryptographers to use

Helmuth Johann Ludwig von Moltke (1848–1916), also known as Moltke the Younger, was a nephew of Generalfeldmarschall Helmuth Karl Bernhard von Moltke and served as the Chief of the German General Staff from 1906 to 1914.

In 1891, on the death of his uncle, Moltke became aide-de-camp to Kaiser Wilhem II. In 1904 Moltke was made Quartermaster-General; in effect, Deputy Chief of the General Staff. In 1906, he became chief on the retirement of Alfred von Schlieffen.

Tsar Nicholas II of Russia with his physically similar cousin, King George V of the United Kingdom (right), in German military uniforms in Berlin before the war; 1913. The likeness is not surprising; their mothers were sisters.

them. The German Army happily read all the Russian military mail going out over its own, former lines.

Crisis at Berlin!

The Germans were having their own problems back at Berlin, in what was long thought to be a sacrosanct area for them: their minutely planned railway troop mobilization, especially the intricate train timetables that had been "firmly" established in 1905 under the late von Schlieffen. In theory, once the Kaiser gave the all-important order to start, two million Reservist soldiers were called to the colors, reporting to their long designated train depots, where they were uniformed, equipped, armed, put into companies, battalions, and regiments, then linked to cavalry, bicyclists, artillery batteries; cook, postal, and blacksmith wagons (for horses), and the soon-to-be necessary field medical services to treat the wounded. Ideally, all of this vast machinery moved smoothly over long carefully prepared railway timetables to frontier concentration points, where they evolved into massed divisions, corps, armies, and army groups—all ready to invade … France! One expert, writing in 1962, recalled that:

> One army corps alone—out of the total of 40 in the German forces—
> required 170 railway cars for officers, 965 for infantry; 2,960 for cavalry;
> 1,915 for artillery and supply wagons; 6,010 in all, grouped into 140

trains, and an equal number again for their supplies. From the moment the order was given, everything was to move at fixed times according to a schedule precise down to the number of train axles that would pass over a given bridge within a given time. Confident in his magnificent system, Deputy Chief of Staff Gen. Alfred von Waldersee had not even returned to Berlin in 1870… 'There is nothing for us to do.' It was a proud tradition inherited from the elder—or 'Great'—Moltke, who on mobilization day in 1870 was found lying on a sofa reading the novel, *Lady Audley's Secret.*

In 1914, however, Kaiser Wilhelm II—facing the reality of a two-front war—was not at all so calm. Not only were His Majesty's hallowed East Prussian hunting grounds facing Russian defilement, but on political grounds, the Kaiser rightly feared that invading France would bring Great Britain into a war of two Aryan states that neither "wanted"—and he was right, too. In fact, France was now scheduled for a German invasion only because the 1905 Schlieffen Plan had decreed it must be so once Russia and Germany were at war. This had been deemed necessary by the General Staff that felt then that vengeful France would never stand aside neutral while the two larger eastern antagonists slugged it out to the death. She would, rather, seize the chance offered by Wilhelm's being distracted in the east, and fall upon the thus vulnerable Reich from its rear, in the west.

Now, every minute was precious, with the German Army moving inexorably on to the French border. The Kaiser knew that Great Britain would not again stand by and see France crushed, as she had in 1870. Now she rightly feared that a German victory on the Continent would inevitably lead to a cross-Channel invasion of the British Isles by a conquest mad German emperor. Now—as Wilhelm worried—the first hostile act in the west was slated to occur within the hour, the capture of a rail junction in Luxembourg, the neutrality of which had been guaranteed by the five Great Powers that included Germany. A flustered Kaiser demanded that it be stopped immediately, having his General Staff Chief re-summoned back to the Imperial Presence, to whom he shouted in great agitation, "We can go to war against Russia only! We simply march our whole army to the east!" For only the second—and also the last—time in his military career, von Moltke the Younger stood up to his emperor, saying no. He had planned for this very moment in history for the last decade day and night, and on that night of 1 August 1914, he was not about to reverse the movement of their forces from west to east on their 11,000 trains. He again faced down Wilhelm II:

Your Majesty, it cannot be done! The deployment of millions cannot be improvised! If Your Majesty insists on leading the whole army to the east, it will not be an army ready for battle, but a disorganized mob of armed men with no arrangements for supply. Those arrangements took a whole year of intricate labor to complete…and once settled, it *cannot* be altered!

Almost immediately—but quietly at first—there were discordant voices on Moltke's own staff who disputed his argument: it could be done, as there even existed in the Bendlerstrasse's files an alternate plan that was not committed to Moltke's expressed "strike France first mantra." This envisioned exactly what the Kaiser proposed, and had been revised and updated every year to 1913: to strike Russia first and only, with all the troop trains running eastward, and not to the west. Thus—without knowing it—His Majesty was right. As a militarily trained commissioned officer himself since he was 10 years old, then Prince Wilhelm had even worked in the Bendlerstrasse learning his craft as a lowly second lieutenant. He knew very well that the German railways were under total military control, even with a designated staff officer in charge of every single line. Indeed, not a single track could be laid or even changed without express General Staff fiat. Since he had attended every annual fall military maneuvers for most of his life, he also realized that these detailed war games were designed for the very flexibility that he was now demanding. Noted one witticism of the period, "The best brains of the War College went into the railway section, and wound up in lunatic asylums." Postwar—when Moltke's memoirs were published in his self-defense against having lost the war at its very outset—Gen. von Staab was outraged at his former chief's assertion to His Majesty that, "It cannot be done!" He saw that as a slur against his command that he refused to brook, writing his own treatise noting how, indeed, it could have been done just as the Kaiser demanded. Publishing charts and graphs, the incensed railway general demonstrated how—had he only been asked on that critical 1 August 1914!—he could and would have deployed four of the seven armies not west, but eastward by 15 August 1914, even leaving three to defend the west against then still un-invaded France and neutral England.

Reportedly—according to Reichstag Deputy and Catholic Center Party leader Matthias Erzberger—a sheepish and then fired von Moltke even admitted that such was true to him, that he secretly had agreed with His Majesty that attacking France at all was a mistake:

> The larger part of our army ought first to have been sent East to smash the Russian steamroller, limiting operations in the West to beating off the enemy's attack on our frontier.

That all-important night of 1 August 1914, however, von Moltke historically chose instead to stand his ground with his consternated Imperial Warlord, causing Wilhelm II against his own better judgment to back down and give way. Enraged, he snapped at him waspishly, "Your uncle would have given me a different answer!"

Imperial Germany declared war on Russia on 1 August 1914 since the Tsar had already partially mobilized and refused to undo it, and on France on the 3rd; this brought a British declaration of war on Germany on the 4th. Thus came the Great War, now recalled as the First World War. One later advanced revisionist premise is that the highly overrated Plan virtually neglected the logistics of supply and re-supply, and that von Moltke actually improved upon "the master's" work. In its final form under Schlieffen—reached during 1897–1905—the Plan allocated 42 days for full mobilization and deployment, with invasions of both Holland and Switzerland, indeed, considered, but abandoned. In order to get at France in 1914, both were discarded in favor of performing a "great wheel" through neutral Belgium instead, thus bringing Great Britain into the war on the side of the Allies. In addition, von Moltke's great wheeling maneuver did not fully succeed. The German CGS then opted to disembark his men from their trains on the entire line Metz–Wesel, reportedly to make fuller use of all the German double trackage heading toward the Reich's western frontier with France.

The Army High Command had by 1914, 90 companies of trained railway troops, but even these would not be enough during the actual operations to keep the military railways running, and Germany's civilian rail personnel had to be called upon for help as well. These—plus the existing Army motor transport and the militarized civilian transportation sector—got the German Army to the First Battle of the Marne in September 1914. As for the railway troops, they had all the requisite *Bauzuge* [Building or Construction Trains] that transited the items necessary for the repair of damaged tracks and also the laying of new ones. These elite specialist units both marched with the advance troops, or actually went before them, as earlier.

The re-supply of fodder for the Army's horses became the major problem, followed by ammunition, with food being next, forcing the men to live off the land, just as von Schlieffen had, indeed, foreseen. Von Moltke took over from von Schlieffen as Chief of Staff on 1 November 1906, and held sway there for the next eight years. He brought with him as his deputy Wilhelm Groener, and both of them together began working on the unsolved logistical problems left behind by their predecessor. It was conceded that, once operations got underway in the field, it would then be necessary for their armies to halt for their supplies to catch up with them, since there were bottlenecks at the railheads where the trains stopped. Sometimes light, narrow gauge rail would suffice to get the men and supplies to the front, and sometimes not. Moltke therefore modified Schlieffen's "great wheel" into a smaller one. For this, he would be much criticized postwar in the memoirs of the 1920s and '30s, for having lost the war at its very outset—August–September 1914—from which the German Army was never able to regain its prior initiative.

Conversely, the Kaiser would be blamed for having both politically allowed—and then brought on—the no-win, two-front war that resulted in both eastern and western theaters, a cardinal, strategic error. In retrospect, one authority considered this comparison:

> In August 1870, nine double-tracked lines served to deploy 350,000 German troops in 15 days, so that 2,580 men rode each line, each day; 44 years later, 13 lines brought up 1,500,000 men … in 10 days, making 11,530 men per day, per line… The effectives of a corps had risen by 50 percent, from 31,000 to 46,000 men.

Not everything that occurred in 1914, was a mistake, and von Moltke the Younger can still be justly credited for what he did achieve then, as well as excoriated for what he did not.

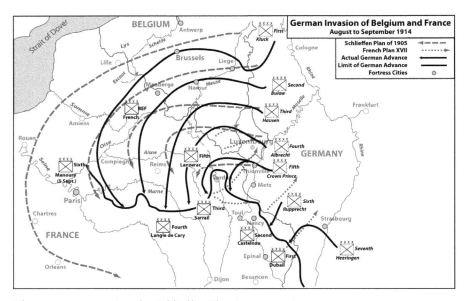

The attempt at putting the Schlieffen Plan into operation.

The Austro-Hungarian Railway Factor, 1879–1918

Considering how badly Prussia had crushed the Austro-Hungarian Army in 1866—and also how easily it had been done as well—it is amazing that the victorious new Teutonic Reich wanted her as a future ally at all, much less to launch a world war in order to honor its pact with her in 1914 over a minor power like Serbia. In *The Forgotten War*, historian Winston Churchill noted that the Battle of Tannenberg:

> Occupied less than a fifth of all troops engaged at that time in the east ... It is curious that so little regard should have been accorded to the other four fifths ... A good part of the work that procured [the German victory at Tannenberg] was done by the Austro-Hungarian Army in the south.

The two major characters in the Germano-Austrian alliance of 1914 were their chiefs of General Staff—von Moltke the Younger for the Reich and Gen. Franz Baron Conrad von Hötzendorff for the Dual Monarchy. Both operated at cross-purposes with the other from start to finish in peace and war. The Austro-Hungarian Army wanted to crush Serbia first, and then to fight the larger foe the Russian Army. The Germans both urged and believed that its hapless ally and former defeated foe would hold Russia in the east, and simply ignore Serbia until the German Army could beat France, and then itself turn east with all its armed might at one throw. Both believed that the other knew its goals, approved of them, and would act accordingly. Neither ally behaved as it was expected to. Rather, the Austrian High Command ignored the Russian Army in the main, invaded Serbia instead, and was itself badly beaten by the Serbian Army at the very outset of the war, thus leaving German East Prussia to fend for itself.

In East Prussia, the German 8th Army faced a Russian military machine that it believed would not act first, as it did. Meanwhile, the Austrian Army in Polish Galicia occupied by the Russians—von Moltke believed—would attack first and beat the Russian Army in southern Poland, but it never happened. Conversely—after the German Army beat France in a projected six-week-long campaign—it would rush reinforcements eastward to beat the Russians *for* Austria. Even as this strategy collapsed, however, the new Duo of Paul von Hindenburg and Ludendorff instead won the most spectacular Great War defensive battle of all, and yet the German reinforcements expected by Austria in August 1914 did not arrive until spring 1915.

Bismarck signed his defensive pact with Austria's Kaiser Franz Josef in 1879, 13 years after the Battle of Sadowa-Königgrätz, with talks between their two General Staffs really only starting in 1882 concerning a projected

Field Marshal Franz Xaver Joseph Conrad Graf von Hötzendorf (1852–1925), was Chief of the General Staff of the armed forces of the Austro-Hungarian Army and Navy 1906–1917. Hötzendorf failed to realise that Germany would force him to put his chief assets on the Russian front, rather than Serbia. Conrad was reluctant to fight Russia, and when Italy entered the war in 1915, he shifted his attention away from Russia toward Italy, the Balkans and the Adriatic.

Above left: Field Marshal Conrad Graf von Hötzendorf. *Above right*: Karl Franz Joseph Ludwig (1887–1922), Emperor of Austria 1916-18 to the left with Hötzendorf to the right. The new Emperor Karl in 1917 dismissed Hötzendorf as Chief of Staff in 1917.

An Austro-Hungarian train in Galicia in 1915. *Library of Congress*

Austrian reservists on their way to war.

German soldiers in East Prussia.
Bundesarchiv

Austro-Hungarian Army defensive line in the Carpathian Mountains. In 1891, von Schlieffen became German CGS, and six years later added his famous dictum that—in order to beat France—the German Army must first invade Belgium on the way into France. The year before, Schlieffen asked the-then Austrian CGS—Gen. Beck—to directly defend "Prussian" Silesia, the very former Austrian province that Frederick the Great had simply stolen from Vienna in 1740. Gen. Beck indignantly rejected this strategy out of hand. Originally, Schlieffen wanted to invade neutral Holland as well, but then decided against it, to have an economic and diplomatic window to the west that was not a battleground. Did Kaiser Wilhelm II plump down for this omission as well, looking ahead to a day when—if defeated—he might need a bordering safe haven from which to seek asylum?

Aping the Russians, so, too, did the Hungarians have their own railroad gauge. In 1914, there was no speedy, direct rail linkage from Vienna to Bosnia, except through Budapest, the capital of Hungary. Indeed, to travel from Ljubljana in Austro-Slovenia to Zagreb in then Hungarian Croatia took three hours to cross but 40 miles. According to the Austrian Archduke—and in 1916, Kaiser—Karl's biographer, Lorenz:

> The Archduke ... when returning from his honeymoon in Dalmatia in 1911, had to transfer from his own state coach to one specifically brought down from the Hungarian capital, since the Hungarian State Railways could accommodate only such a carriage.

At length, the 1909–14 proportion of the German Army to be deployed in the west of all its forces available stood at 8/9ths, with but 13 divisions of the 8th German Army deployed to guard the East Prussian frontier with Tsarist Russia. In addition, the German 8th Army facing the Russian Army on their common frontier, there was, an army corps of inexperienced soldiers loosely attached to the left wing of the allied (Austro-German) army. As noted by Norman Stone in 1966:

> The exact strength of the Austro-Hungarian Army in 1914 was 48 infantry and 11 cavalry divisions, two *Landsturm*/militia divisions, and 41 reserve brigades. The German Army contained 90 infantry and 11 cavalry divisions.

In any German–Russian conflict, republican France would not stand idly by as the Reich vanquished the French ally to the East, Russia, but would attack Imperial Germany in the west—or so that untested theory went. Meanwhile, Moltke the Younger said nothing of Belgium to Gen. Conrad; ridiculed their then joint ally the Royal Italian Army and wrongly predicted that the Tsar would not intervene against Austria over his fellow Slavs—the Serbs being conquered by Vienna. In addition, Moltke confirmed Conrad's worst fear: that few German troops would be moved eastward either at or in the first few months of an Eastern Front war. In contrast, Conrad wanted 10 German Army divisions crossing the Narev River into then-Russian Poland as the start of any such projected joint future Austro-German War with Russia. If so, Conrad was then willing to attack Russia with 30 Austro-Hungarian divisions, with the Germans beating the Russian Army of the Narev (as the Duo did in 1914), and the Austro-Hungarians following suit by attacking in southern Poland. Threatening to stand aside if not in the east, Moltke mollified Conrad by lying that Germany would attack first from East Prussia, but did not.

Moltke in 1914 was entirely focused on his Western Front, believing as he did that the entire war would be settled there—and in the end, he was right. On the River Seine would be decided the fate of battles on the Rivers Vistula, Drina, and Bug all. On one thing both Moltke and Conrad did agree, that their unreliable Triple Alliance partner Savoyard Italy had a negligible army, and also that she would change sides and fight with their enemies the Allies, as happened during 1915–16. As with Prussia in 1866, so also had the Italians beaten the Austrians. Another hoped for and reluctant partner was Rumania, but she also joined the Allies in 1916, only to be overrun by the Germans. Another point on which the two chiefs of General Staff agreed was of an "eventual" Germano-Slavic war, or *Germanentum versus Slaventum*, as occurred twice.

Moltke failed to confide in Conrad that he reckoned as well with England joining the French and maybe Russia, but only after two full years of war elapsed. In this, he was glaringly proven wrong.

A few weeks prior to August 1914, the two chiefs met at Karlsbad Spa in Austrian Bohemia, and Moltke frankly admitted to his opposite number that, "We are not superior to the French!" in numbers. On 28 July 1914, Austria declared war on Serbia, with Wilhelm II already having issued his diplomatic "blank check" to stand at Austria's side no matter what occurred. Already at war with Serbia, Conrad also wanted to fight Russia as well, and on 25 July 1914, he had partially mobilized his forces, but to fight Serbia alone then. It is still hotly debated whether or not he believed that the Tsar would allow Vienna to vanquish his Serbian Slav cousins. In the campaign at Limberg in the east, the Austrians had captured prisoners from both Siberian and Caucasian units that could hardly—due to the Russians' known sizable transportation problems—have reached their western front if mobilization had occurred only at the end of July 1914 as the Tsar's officials maintained; they had been called up earlier. On 31 July 1914, Wilhelm II sent Franz Josef this urgent telegram: "It is of primary importance that Austria should mobilize her main forces against Russia, and not fragment herself through any simultaneous offensive on Serbia." The Austrians did just as they pleased, showing both disdain and even contempt for their "ally" who had humiliated Vienna both in 1740 and 1866. Meanwhile, their own Army railway section chief advised the delay

Kaiser Wilhelm and Helmuth von Moltke.

of any Austrian mobilization against their former Napoleonic Wars ally, Russia.

There was an odd comparison between Germany and Austria as well during the very same period in summer 1914. Just as Kaiser Wilhelm II raged against Moltke to switch all trains away from still peaceful France and toward Russia instead, so, also at Vienna Conrad balked at switching his forces from Serbia and against Russia instead, over the wishes of his Sovereign, Kaiser Franz Josef. In his postwar memoirs Conrad stated:

> On 31 July 1914, it was impossible to send the Austrian 2nd Army to Galicia; it had already started for Serbia, and it could not be reversed without causing chaos in the mobilization.

Had Moltke and Conrad written in advance rehearsed answers to the expected demands of their respective emperors? One wonders. Worse still, Conrad also told His Majesty:

> It must continue its predestined course to the Serbian Front and—having arrived there—depart again for the Galician Front, when the mobilization lines are clear …

and thus, might have been reversed as desired two days earlier.

> Now, however, the transports to Serbia were already in movement. To interrupt them at short notice would have caused—[again]—chaos.

In fact, all Conrad had done was to parrot to His Majesty the pat answers given to him by his railway section chief, Lt-Col. Straub of the Austro-Hungarian General Staff. Asserted Straub to Conrad, and Conrad to Franz Josef, "This would be a catastrophe for which I can take no responsibility!" At that moment only 15,000 soldiers were actually *en route* for the Serbian battlefront. They both could and would have been reversed had the order been given.

Conrad had asserted that July, "The Serbian War proceeds with all energy, and we turn against Russia after striking down Serbia with rapid blows!" The opposite happened. By 31 July 1914, the neutrality of both Italy and Rumania had been confirmed, and on 4 August 1914, Bulgaria also determined to "wait and see" how the German Army fared in France before making any decision. Moltke reneged on his promise to Conrad to attack the Russians at the outset, leading the Austrian CGS to recall his 2nd Army from Galicia. By 6 August 1914, Moltke reversed himself on his Kaiser's direct command, with the new Duo about to end the Cossack sweep of East Prussia with fire and sword.

Ironically, Conrad ordered the exact re-deployment in the east as had Moltke in the west, belatedly sending his 2nd Army from Serbia to Galicia. Posited Churchill afterwards, "It left (Gen. Oskar) Potiorek before it could win him a victory" over the Serbs; and "it returned to Conrad in time to participate in his defeat" by the Russians. It never was, its army was beaten, and the dynasty itself fell in late 1918. Conrad's attack against the Russian Army in southern Poland occurred during 23 August–11 September 1914, when it was halted at the Battle of Lemberg by the Russian Army, and an Austro-Hungarian retreat was ordered instead at almost the precise moment as Moltke commenced his own withdrawal after losing the First Battle of the Marne River in France—5 p.m. 11 September 1914.

Opening Act: Belgian Railways Captured Virtually Intact by Germany

Great Britain declared war on Imperial Germany in 1914 because German victory would have meant the Kaiser dominating Europe. In the Middle East, German control of the Persian Gulf via the Berlin to Baghdad Railway would have posed the very same threat to British India.

Surprisingly—in the face of the Belgian Army's laxity—the Germans basically took over that invaded country's railways, transporting both men and supplies over Belgian territory. The swiftness of the German advance into their stricken land caused the Belgians to be unable to completely destroy their railroads, but not for at least some lack of trying. In addition to the usual track destruction, there were at least 17 known instances of simply crashing engines into one another, but the German railway troops repaired these rather quickly even so. Working 24 hours a day—they had traffic running again to Landen on 22 August 1914, to Louvain on the 24th, at Cambrai six days further on, and to St-Quentin by 4 September 1914. Despite this, though, sometimes the nearest points of supply were 85 miles to the front's rear, and until Ludendorff forced the surrender of Liège, there appeared there a bottleneck that both glutted troops and supplies and froze them in position. The upper part of Ans-Liège saw trackage so high that it needed four locomotive engines to propel the trains onward. An accident at Ans occurred on 23 August 1914 with a resultant state of continual crisis along the very railway that needed to support the main German advance cross-country.

The German Army had planned on taking intact four distinct Belgian lines for their five right wing armies. One was to follow Gen. Alexander von Kluck via Liège, Louvain, and Brussels that fell on 20 August 1914, and then on to Cambrai, for logistical support of the 1st Army. A second

Big Bertha at the siege of Liège.

Alexander Heinrich Rudolph von Kluck (1846–1934) was made a general of infantry in 1906, and in 1913 was appointed Inspector General of the Seventh Army District. With the outbreak of war I, Kluck was placed in command of the German First Army on the Western Front.

line was to run southwest from Liège to Namur to supply the 2nd and 3rd Armies, while the 4th and 5th at the center of the great wheel were to be supplied by a pair of lines via Luxembourg, proceeding on to Libramount–Namur, plus a line Metz–Sedan also operational. However, the 26,000 men of the railway construction companies were unable to cope with Belgian and French railroad sabotage by mid-September 1914, and found themselves serving guard duty to protect these lines. Another problem was that individual Army commanders along the lines simply hijacked passing trains for their own usage, they never reaching their intended destinations. One report stated:

> So-called 'wild' wagons loaded with well-meant presents to the troops, were often sent back from railheads unable to receive them, and would then roam the network with little or no control from above.

And yet—despite all of the known railway travail of the above, just as before during 1866–71—there remains little to show that German trains in any way caused the Army's all-important defeat on the River Marne that was the western war's first real benchmark of overall success or failure as a campaign. It was a distinct bust, an outcome that had been totally unforeseen at Berlin, just as had the earlier unexpected swiftness and impact of the Russian Army's invasion of East Prussia. Even more remarkable—and, again, just as during 1866–71—had the German Army won that epic fight instead of lost it, their own high-precision railway plans would still have then hindered them from the further occupation of France via a pursuit of the beaten French Army on to Paris and beyond. One authority presented this statistic:

> In 1914, it took 240 trains—with 50 cars each—to transport two German Army corps … It was impossible to transport troops forward from Aix-la-Chapelle by rail. Only one double-tracked line was available to 1st and 2nd armies, and this could handle only some 24 trains per day, of which four were needed for the operation of the railways themselves. To bring up the fighting elements of two corps, 120 trains were required....

A century later, there is still no real data as to trainloads transiting the captured Belgian railways, nor the actual numbers, condition, and siting of the Belgian stations that were employed. Operationally, the much-touted 1905 Schlieffen Plan in the actual event of 1914 was proving impractical to put into execution on the ground in France—the very country it was designed for. More simply put, the mammoth German Army of two million men of 1914 was just too big to move with all the various means at hand to do so—foot, horseback, motor cars and trucks, and railroad lines combined. In the opinion of one railway expert:

> Had a few tunnels been blown up along Kluck's route, the entire campaign would have been utterly impossible.

The Germans failed to prepare for that ever-present factor in all wartime military operations: the unexpected.

Hindenburg and Ludendorff Meet on a Railway Platform, 23 August 1914

At the outset of the war, the Russians advanced with fire and sword in ravaged East Prussia that August of 1914 amid German cries of, "The Cossacks are coming!" reaching the anguished Kaiser in Berlin. A new German Army commander and chief of staff for the Eastern Front were duly appointed to rectify the situation. Neither man had met the other, however, and one—von Hindenburg, 66—was called out of retirement to lead the force. From his Hanoverian home, the stolid, dour, massively-built von Hindenburg telegraphed his brief reply—"I am ready"—when at 3 p.m. that day he had received an earlier telegram asking him to take command of the floundering German 8th Army in East Prussia. A follow-up message ordered him to leave immediately for the now raging Eastern Front by taking a train from Hanover. It also informed him that his new chief of staff—Gen. Ludendorff—would meet him *en route*. Meanwhile, the latter arrived at Koblenz at 6 p.m., and at nine boarded a special train eastward, stopping on the way at Hanover to pick up his new commanding officer. This train consisted of a trio of carriages: a sleeping car living area for each, and the third a combined office/dining car. Ludendorff sat alone as the train glided into Hanover Station at 4 a.m., 23 August 1914, where Hindenburg awaited its arrival on the platform, one of military history's most famous duos about to be joined. Once aboard, Ludendorff detailed the actions he had already ordered on "their" behalf, setting the regimen at the very outset of their unique partnership that would last through to its end in Belgium more than four years later. From it was also born their later famous iconic monogram that joined together the first letters of each of their last names, H and L, or HL.

Hindenburg's account of 1920 noted in his postwar memoirs:

> The short, special train steamed in … Gen. Ludendorff stepped briskly
> from the train and reported as my chief of staff … Before long, I and

Above left: *Left:* Paul Ludwig Hans Anton von Beneckendorff und von Hindenburg (1847–1934) and Erich Friedrich Wilhelm Ludendorff (1865–1937).

Above right: Hindenburg retired in 1911, but was recalled shortly after the outbreak of war. He was the victor of the decisive Battle of Tannenberg in August 1914. As Germany's Chief of the General Staff from August 1916, Hindenburg's reputation rose greatly in German public esteem. He and his deputy Erich Ludendorff would then lead Germany in a *de facto* military dictatorship throughout the remainder of the war, marginalizing Wilhelm II as well as the German Reichstag.

Field Marshal Paul von Hindenburg receives a bouquet of welcoming flowers during a wartime station stop. He served as Chief of the Great German General Staff during 1916–18, and here wears the Blue Max and Grand Cross of the Iron Cross medals at the throat, with crossed batons on his shoulder boards as well. During the war, he supplanted the Kaiser both in wartime propaganda and public opinion as the real leader of the Reich's war effort. *Library of Congress*

my new chief of staff were at one in our view of the situation … Our conference had taken scarcely more than half an hour. We then went to bed.

 The top priority train sped eastward past stations and over points. It rode past all manner of other trains steaming eastward as well: troop transports bedecked with flowers from their departed platforms back home, full ammunition freight cars, cavalry horses, and artillery pieces, all destined for the first Eastern Front. They reached the famous East Prussian town of Marienburg—with its towering, red-bricked, medieval fortress—at 2 p.m. on 24 August 1914, just 11 hours after Hindenburg had first received word of what was to be his most famous field command. Awaiting the new "Duo" on its railway platform was two of their most important subordinates: Col. Max Hoffmann, and Maj-Gen. Paul Grünert. On the afternoon of the 22nd, the Eastern Front Director of Railways— Maj-Gen. Kersten—strode into Col. Hoffmann's office to announce the coming arrival of the pair of new top officers, and in this haphazard way, the now fired CO Gen. Maximilian von Prittwitz and his chief of staff Maj-Gen. Alfred von Waldersee offhandedly were informed of their own abrupt firings.

   Now the Duo were broiling on their special train as an ersatz field headquarters for 8th Army, joined by Col. Hoffmann and others, as all worked under the hot metal roofs of the carriages. There was still bad blood between the two main Russian Army commanders—Samsonov and Rennenkampf—left over from the Russo-Japanese War of 1904–05, when they had reportedly slugged it out on a railway platform at Mukden in the Far East, according to then eyewitness Hoffmann. The stage was set for the great German victory and corresponding mammoth Russian defeat of the epic Battle of Tannenberg. Unfortunately for the Germans, their additional two army corps reinforcements shipped by rail from west to east failed to reach that battlefield in time, they also being denied to the German Army in France, simultaneously thereby leading to the Germanic defeat at the pivotal First Battle of the Marne. The Duo shifted their mobile train headquarters further east over then conquered Russian Poland to Kovno on 20 October 1915, and on 1 August 1916, left there for Brest-Litovsk. Their train was once more shunted onto a siding, wherein huge campaign maps took up most of its cramped space aboard, at what Ludendorff glumly termed, "The ugly but highly important railway junction. The gutted town offered few attractions."

   On 28 August 1916—two years after they had first come east—the Duo boarded their train at 4 p.m. "We left Brest," wrote Ludendorff, ''never again to return to the Eastern Front. Behind us lay two years of

Hindenburg and Ludendorff at their headquarters in Bad Kreuznach, 2 October 1917.

Above left: Aleksandr Vassilievich Samsonov (1859–1914) was a general during the Russo-Japanese War and the First World War. His army was trapped in a German encirclement; the German Eighth Army killed or captured most of his troops. Only 10,000 of the 150,000 Russian soldiers managed to escape the encirclement. Shocked by the disastrous outcome of the battle Samsonov committed suicide on 30 August 1914.

Above right: Paul von Rennenkampf (1854–1918) was a Russian general who served in the Imperial Russian Army for over 40 years, including during the First World War. Rennenkampf was given command of the Russian First Army for the invasion of East Prussia, advancing from the northeast. His failure to coordinate with Alexander Samsonov's Second Army, resulted in much criticism from sector commander General Yakov Zhilinskiy and attempts by some members of the military high command to have him removed from command.

strenuous, united work, and mighty victories." They had been summoned by His Majesty the Kaiser to Imperial GHQ at Castle Pless to assume the supreme military command of Germany's war effort, as Wilhelm II's favorite commander— Gen. Erich von Falkenhayn—had been forced to resign.

The Western Front, 1914

French troops from Amiens were re-routed north after Paris, with the country's railways already clogged once again, but this time by the happy and speedy arrival in France of the promised and now delivered British Expeditionary Force [BEF] from across the English Channel, come to jointly fight the surging, gray-clad "Huns." The BEF landed in France, later detraining at Amiens on 26 August 1914. Unlike Hindenburg, Ludendorff had begun his Great War, meanwhile, on 2 August 1914, when he entrained with his horses at Strasbourg early on a Sunday morning via Cologne for Belgium. He watched with satisfaction as packed troops trains passed through at the rate of one every 10 minutes, all bound northward like him for the treaty-breaking German invasion of that unhappy land. This was being done in order to better attack belligerent France. Once in Belgium, Ludendorff became the celebrated "Hero of Liège" by allegedly banging on the city gates of the Belgian fortress with the pommel of his sword, demanding—and getting—its surrender. The previous war of movement ground to a halt in the west during 1914–16. Meanwhile—on the Eastern Front—the Duo achieved one dazzling martial victory after another over the Russians, none of which ended the war there. In summer 1916, Hindenburg was named Chief of the General Staff by the Kaiser, with Ludendorff as his First Quartermaster General, in charge of the overall war effort. In fall 1917, Ludendorff's command train had an accident, and his personal coach was rolled over. He survived the event, and finished his front inspection tour. By then, literally hundreds of trains were transporting many thousands of troops to this most important theater of the entire Great War for both sides. Despite all the Duo's best efforts, by 1918, British arms laid waste roads, railroads, bridges, and tunnels, with German divisions stranded miles in advance of their supply trains, units running out of ammunition, and no more coming. The end for Imperial Germany was near. How had the German Army's cherished and long planned former war of movement in the west gone awry in fall 1914, unable to be reversed by the Duo two years later, and then been ground down to defeat overall across four bitter years of a war it had expected to win outright? It has been hotly debated ever since.

From Railway Mobilizations to the First Battle of the Marne, 1914

Norton in his 1915 *Report* wrote:

> At the outbreak of the Great War, the strategic railways that Germany had constructed towards, along, and jointly with the Belgian government (owing to the pressure she had brought to bear upon them)—even across the Belgian frontier—enabled her at once to concentrate and to throw into that country great masses of troops for an invasion of France. But although these railways afforded her material aid in rushing troops on to Belgian territory, Germany had not anticipated so vigorous an opposition at Liège by the brave-hearted Belgians, who thus thwarted her design, first to make a sudden descent on France by rail, and then, to rush the main body of her troops, also by rail, back through Germany for the attack on Russia. From a railway point of view, the action taken by Belgium was of exceptional value to the Allies, since it meant that— although Germany crossed the frontiers of Belgium and Luxembourg on 3 August 1914—it was not until the 24th that she was in a position to attack the French Army, which by that time had not only completed both its mobilization and its concentration, but had been joined by the first arrivals of the BEF... When ... the Belgian opposition had been effectively crushed, the close network of railways in that country became a powerful auxiliary to Germany's further operations against France.

But the Second Reich's concentration on the usage of its own railway grid plus that added by the other captured train lines that included those of Luxembourg, caused the General Staff to underestimate the capacity of both the French, and then the BEF, wartime railways upon the Continent. The defeated French Army military railways of 1871 had been vastly improved by 1914 up to the Franco-German frontier, and also by cross-country line linkage to provide both a smooth mobilization at the outset of the war and then subsequent field concentration. The French had truly learned the brutal lessons of 1870–71. Upon the Second Reich's 31 July 1914 "danger of war" proclamation by the Kaiser—the French military railway system had in place its ready response. They met the invading German Army by noon of 3 August 1914 in the first armed clash—the Battle of the Frontiers—even though French civil rail traffic continued on as before; 600 troop trains roared eastward to meet the hated *Boche* [Cabbage or blockhead] in mortal combat. The French general mobilization began on 2 August 1914, with troops soon being sped on their way east to concentration points via the French Army's own railroad timetables during 5–19 August 1914, over two weeks. Almost 4,500 troop trains were deployed, aside from 250 more transiting supplies to French frontier forts barring the way westward from the Reich into France. Once achieved, a grateful French government at Paris issued public thanks for all French railway officers and workmen, top to bottom, for having saved France. On 30 January 1915, the *Journal of Transport* announced that, "One can justly say that the first victory" (the Marne) "in this great conflict has been won by the railway men!"

Norton continued with his *Report* the following year:

No sooner was the concentration of France's seven armies—six along the Front and one in Paris—accomplished, than the railways had to ensure between 12–20 August, the conveyance to Mons of the officers and men of the BEF, who had by that time arrived at Boulogne, Nantes, and St Nazaire. This alone involved the running of 420 transport trains. Provision had to be made ... for the transport across France from Marseilles of 60,000 (black colonial) French troops from Africa, and also of the troops arriving there from (British) India. The masterly retreat of the Allied center and right to south of the Marne River— that followed the fall of Charleroi on 26 August 1914—called for an especially prodigious effort on the part of the French railways. This effort—crowned with complete success—had to be made concurrently with the need for facilitating the flight of many thousands of refugees from the invaded or threatened districts of Belgium and northern France.... there was secured for the defense of Paris so speedy and so strong a re-concentration of the Allied forces that not only was the advance of the (German) invaders checked, but the enemy was himself thrown back in some disorder successively to the Petit Morin, the Marne River, and the Aisne River. The first great object of the German invasion failed, and Paris was saved.

There was to be no repeat of 1870, with the last Kaiser never riding in triumph into the surrendered French capital as had both his father and grandfather. Still, the French government left Paris for Bordeaux, from which to continue the war if, indeed, their real capital had fallen in 1914 yet again. This removal to Bordeaux was likewise joined by the Parisian population, plus a continued exodus from both Belgium and northern France. In 1966, a French memoirist recalled the 1914 French mobilization:

The 3,400 trains carrying troops through the length and breadth of the country were gay with flags and flowers. Peasants in the fields would wave as these convoys went by. They drew into stations in a long, cheering, happy line to an uproarious welcome. The men in them were seized upon, embraced, loaded with gifts and flowers, with sausages and kisses, and glasses of wine. Crowds gathered—even at the wayside halts—shouting, 'Long live France! Long live the Army!' The youngsters called out, 'Come back soon!' and the soldiers answered, 'We will be back in two months' time!' Women held up their children like an offering to the gods. An entire population had taken leave of its senses.

The fall of Liège to Ludendorff made of this Belgian fortress city a new and now major German Army train hub connecting in theory Berlin–Brussels–Paris. Despite its later criticisms, overall, the German Army's long-planned railway mobilization had been the success meticulously projected in 1905. The initial near-three weeks of the German mobilization projected at least 20,800 trains bearing a complement of 50 cars apiece that carried 2.07 million men; plus nearly 20,000 horses, and 400,000 tons of front-bound various war materials. Each and every German Army corps had its own 140 trains, 85 being assigned to each Reserve corps, and 31 more for every cavalry division. For the westbound trek alone, there were earmarked 13 major railroad lines, with an astounding 660 trains daily humming along each one. Moltke's schedule budgeted but 40 days for the next Fall of France, and then he would do what His Majesty had wanted on 1 August 1914: reverse course and send them all hurtling east to beat the Tsar's "slower" gathering forces. But it all worked out quite differently.

Aside from his patently incorrect estimate that the shattered Russian Army of 1905 would need at least 40 days itself to complete its own General Mobilization, the SP was proven wrong when the German Army did not invade neutral Holland when it did Belgium and Luxembourg, and seized its railways. He was mistaken again in his belief that the sudden, surprise German invasion would catch the unaware Allied armies in the west napping; they were not. Finally, he wrongly calculated that the German military train system would have time to shift enough armed weight by rail to forestall any such Russian incursion of East Prussia. Despite all the postwar—mostly Germanic—criticism of the Younger Moltke for his activation and carrying out of the SP—even some German historians have concluded that, "He brilliantly supervised the overall mobilization of the Reich's mammoth and mighty war machine. His Military Telegraph Section at Berlin's several large post offices oversaw 200,000 telegraphers and others, plus 100,000 telephone operators who alerted for mobilization the Reich's 106 infantry brigades nationwide for call up for active duty. His Railroad Section of 23 directorates requisitioned 30,000 engines; 65,000 passenger coaches, and an additional 800,000 freight cars used to marshal all 25 active German Army corps." The Reich's long awaited general mobilization was fully underway on 2 August 1914. Under the fine-honed Military Traffic Plan of 312 hours 119,754 officers, 2.1 million enlisted men, and 600,000 horses on 11,000 trains were shipped westward.

Trundling like clockwork over the Rhine River railway bridges, 1.6 million of these men organized in 498 cavalry detachments and 950 infantry battalions rode in an estimated 560 trains of 54 cars apiece for an average rate of speed of 30 kmh to their assigned marshalling yards. At Cologne alone 2,150 such trains roared over the appropriately named Hohenzollern Bridge at incredible 10-minute intervals during 2–8 August 1914—while only as north as the former Imperial city of Aachen—as that was only as far as the German network then reached in its southwestern corner. Lt-Gen. Groener was in charge of the Field Railway Service's 26,000 men, who were required to restore damaged lines connecting Aachen and Liège. Despite his famous surrender to Ludendorff, Belgian Army Gen. Gerard Leman's stout defense at Liège delayed the Germans for two days out of the planned conquest timeframe. As opposed to the 1870 bungling, France's 1914 mobilization ran quite well, with 14 major railroad lines during 2–18 August 1914, handling an average of 56 trains daily for 4,278 in all to the front fortress towns of Sedan, Toul, Nancy, Belfort, and Montmédy railway depots and posted military garrisons, with only 20 not on time; 1.6 million French soldiers reached their Eastern Front at the rate of 25–30 kms daily.

Lt Henri Desagneaux of the French Army railway Transport Service on 4 August 1914 reported the fervor of the pro-war slogans on the trains as the men left for the front: *Death to the Kaiser, String the Kaiser Up, Death to the Boches*, as well as cartoons of pig's heads wearing pointed helmets. The overall French Army commander—Gen. Joseph "Papa" Joffre—used well his own interior railroad lines via the excellent Directorate of Railways, starting on 24 August 1914 to shuttle his battalions north to halt the Germans' all-important right wing wheeling maneuver bearing down on threatened Paris. He sent as reinforcements 109 trains with Gen. Boelle's 4th French Army Corps on 1 September 1914. On the 2nd, the 9th Corps under Gen. Dubois left in 52 trains from Nancy for Troyes, with the Goundecourt-bound 74 trains from Épinal of Gen. Legrande-Girarde—as well as four more divisions from Alsace-Lorraine to beat the Germans outside Greater Paris. As for the Allied BEF's rail mobilization in both England and Ireland, about 1,800 trains ran across five hectic days of embarkation, with 80 reaching the docks of the port of Southampton on the very busiest day alone.

Having run out of draft horses to haul German artillery batteries in the very same way as at Sedan, Gen. Otto Kreppel sent the heavier units via rail—plus

26 trainloads of deadly shells—to Nancy in France. Once again—as in the earlier trio of Prussian wars—the infantry of the German 1st Army simply out-marched its supply trains, with the main depot of Chauny being 140 kms distant from the fighting front by 4 September 1914. Conversely, blue-coated, red-trouser-clad French Army men boarded their designated trains at St-Hilaire-au-Temple, Cuperly, Suippes, and Somme-Suipes, plus one full corps on eight more at Châlons-sur-Marne, and four others at Mairy-sur-Marne. During the night of 7–8 September 1914, French Military Governor of Paris Gen. Joseph Gallieni made one more famous guarantee of Gallic martial victory—in case the railways ran out—by sending the famed Parisian taxicab auto fleet packed with soldiers off to face the Germans. Despite the legend, though, one noted German history authority asserts that "much" of the French infantry, artillery, and staff left Gay Paree not via this much-celebrated means, but via the more standard railroad cars. A better railway commander than Moltke the Younger, Papa Joffre shunted forces right to left on the broad front facing the "Huns" via tracks, moving a full corps of between 105–118 trains over four-six days, making Joffre the true railway victor of 1914 via his French Directorate of Railways, not Germany's.

Having lost the opening Battle of the Frontiers to the Germans, Joffre redeemed himself by winning the most important battle of the entire war on the Marne River, thus halting the German drive on his capital, and saving Paris for the first of two times that it was so rescued during the Great War.

Due to observant air corps services of all the combatant armies during the Great War, no surprise railway attacks were possible. Seven miles behind the battlefront, British military railroads were a far cry as well from those of 1870–71. The Germans used their light, 60 cm field railways in Continental Europe as well as in Africa. This, in turn, led the BEF to establish its own directorate of light railways during 1915–16. These so-called toy town railways suffered many derailments, however. Even so, these lighter railroads had a large role in the maintenance of effective communication. Most traffic was at night towards war's end—with small lights, and no timetables, while telephone posts near the lines provided some control. These night trains had a crew of three: driver, fireman, and sentry/brake operator, with about 100–150 such trains running. With almost all lines being single track, it was up to the drivers of opposing directional trains as to who would back off into a loop or siding to let the rival pass!

Both men and supplies were transported, with the Allies deploying 132 American Ford Model-T automobiles mounted on the tracks as ersatz railway cars! By December 1915, there was a growing shortage of French Army railway men and rolling stock, and this reached crisis proportions by January 1916. During the climactic Battle of Verdun that

Men, munitions and duck boards for the trenches is squeezed into light railway wagons on the British side of the front.

Coming in the other direction, wounded are lain onto flat hand trucks.

Canadian soldiers on a light railway heading for the showers.

A British light railway with a gasoline vehicle converted to rail use.

Canadians being evacuated along a light railway route.

year, French Gen. Henri Pétain stationed cavalry along the rail lines to protect his supply lines. Horses protected the six 60 cm light railway lines that supplied a battle lasting 10 months with two million troops and 300,000 casualties, an interesting juncture of both Nineteenth and Twentieth Century warfare. As winter 1916–17 arrived, French railway trains had increased by 50 percent from their peacetime levels, but a good deal of these 14,000 engines could not run, due to few spare parts and repair crews. The British provided France with 300 new standard issue new engines, with 500 more from the United States. Also in 1917, plans began for more Allied light rail to be deployed, and by March 1918, there existed 1,000 light railway lines laid and 150 Allied tramway lines, with an expected even larger counterpart on the German side of the trenches. The German Army maintained a huge reserve of 60 cm gauge engines, with more than 2,500 steam locomotives alone, deployed most notably in Poland on the Eastern Front, where Imperial Germany won that part of the Great War.

The AEF started arriving in Europe in the summer of 1917, some two million soldiers with the U.S. Army Transportation Corps of 50,000 troops operating Pershing locomotives in concert with French railway men. Without the efficiency of these railroads, the war might have ended much later. In the last eight months of the Great War, one of mobility resumed such as had not been seen since it ground to a halt in December 1914. In addition, light *Feldbahnen* [Field railways] were hastily executed to service the rival trenches of both sides, as the fighting front became static, with dug-in, crude field fortifications running for hundreds of miles, literally! In the west mainly, they also brought both men and victuals the remaining miles separating rear area railheads from the trench systems.

The Duo on the Western Front, 1916–18

The duo of Hindenburg–Ludendorff inspected the Western Front for the first time on 9 September 1916. As before, the most celebrated pair of soldiers in German military history traveled about in their own special train that was equipped with not only the usual radiotelephones, but also the new telegraphic Hughes Patent Machine. Like their predecessor in high command—Gen. Erich von Falkenhayn—the celebrated, but overrated, Eastern Front Duo could not break the Allies opposite them in the west. In March 1918, Ludendorff launched his last-gasp operation, codenamed *Michael* or *Kaisersschlacht* [Emperor's Battle], the second and final major German attempt to take Paris. His railroad system—extended during previous weeks—ran at full capacity, mostly at night. His Majesty arrived on 19 March 1918, residing in his luxurious special train on an isolated siding. By 24 March 1918, Ludendorff noted:

> The ammunition was not sufficient, and supply became more difficult. The repair of roads and railways was taking too long, in spite of all our preparations.

The battle was lost—and so was the war— but Imperial Germany held on until the fall of 1918 nonetheless.

After Russia withdrew from the war, the German Army rushed 50 Eastern Front divisions of 600,000 men to the Western Front by rail to face the Allies during its last gasp *Michael* offensive of 21 March 1918 that was designed to beat the British at Amiens—a key railway town—push the entire BEF into the English Channel. Despite impressive initial gains by the German Army, it was the Allied infantry who deployed faster via rail than did their enemies on foot, thereby winning the second Battle of the Marne in July 1918, saving Paris again. This drove the beaten Germans to ask for an armistice, the latter being Ludendorff's direct advice to the Kaiser and Hindenburg, who ordered it to be sought. His Majesty fired Ludendorff on 27 October 1918. That same summer, it was the French Army's trains that were in a perilous state once more. The tide turned, when—on 18 August 1918—1.3 million Americans and their Allies launched the final, major push of the war, with multiple stations being used for different

The Kaiser in conference with Hindenburg and Ludendorff in front of detailed maps, 8 January 1917. The GHQ was located in Pless castle in Silesia in order to ensure effective coordination with the Austro-Hungarian allies.

types of supply, and once more, light rail prevailed. By Armistice Day— 11 November 1918—there were advanced Allied railheads all along the Western Front, with the British Army 50 miles ahead of its own.

The so-called "war to end all wars" did not, but, rather, just stopped in place, dead in its tracks, with German troops still occupying conquered French territory, and no enemy soldiers on any part of the Reich's. This later helped to fuel postwar German propaganda that—somehow— the Second Reich really had not lost the Great War at all, but had been instead tricked into making peace by the false promises of American President Woodrow Wilson. As regards its military railways, the official transportation report noted that the growing counter-railroad strength of the Allies in contrast to that of the weakening Germans, played a large part in bringing the war to its conclusion. The railway war on the Western Front ran out of steam for the beaten Germans.

The Eastern Front, 1918

Oddly, the very lack of railroads meant in the end a more mobile war in the East, again as had earlier been the case. One million German soldiers fought on the 1914–16 Eastern Front that stretched 750–1,000 miles, with the Russian Army being pushed out of Poland by 1916. The famous *Brusilov* offensive that started on 4 June 1916 in Ukraine and the Baltics against the Austro-Hungarian Army was halted when the Germans transported four entire corps by rail to the Russian's single corps. It ended on 16 June 1916, with 300,000 casualties inclusive for both sides combined. Russian railways in the main ran east to west, and not north to south. Often railway junctures were fought over in major pitched battles at the axial sites of lines that stayed intact. Taken together, of all the train wars of 1854–1956, the Great War remains the Railway Age's combats as its most destructive by far. Long lines linked disparate frontal segments with one another north to south.

In 1915 came the initial German Army Bulgarian 60 cm line, with more than 200 miles by war's end, some of them still in operation in 1969. Reportedly, the German Army made good usage of all the enemy railways it captured in Central Europe. On conquered territory, the German railway troops repaired damages to tracks in the wake of the retreating Russian Army, but—as much as possible—also re-gauged lengthy portions of the 5′ wide lines to the European standard 4′ 8½″—but never enough. Still—by May 1916—nearly 5,000 such converted trackage stood ready in formerly Russian occupied Poland, Belarus, and Lithuania. It was a matter of narrowing down just 3½″ rather than widening the lines and could be done easier, but the work still delayed the war. Working in freezing weather with iced-up rails, little could be done in wintertime. Not until January 1917 did the Russian Ministry of Transport bring all its myriad lines under its own, central direction, just a month shy of the first Russian Revolution that overthrew its commander-in-chief, Tsar Nicholas II.

Armored Trains

Surprisingly, armored trains played but a small part in the Great War, few being deployed at all in the west, while only a "couple" appeared in Ukraine for the German invasion. Still, the DRG kept some of them ready, just in case they might be needed. The Russian Army had established its own Train Section in 1912, that during the Great War defeated a German Army infantry assault on Lvov that saw taken Koluszki station. By 1916, the Austrian Army had its own reserve of Imperial armored trains, too, with 10 gaining military awards for valuable service versus the enemy armies of Russia, Rumania, and Savoyard Italy. This caused the Russian Army to build 15, the most celebrated of which was *Zaamurets*, all deployed against the German Army in the east until war's end.

An armored train belonging to the Austro-Hungarian Army. Nine of these were built during the war and saw action on all fronts.

The Role of Railways in the African War, 1914–18

Now we turn to the East African jungle and desert war that—although Imperial Germany did not "win"—she also did not "lose" militarily. It was surrendered via the European armistice. Having been the first of the European Great Powers to both recognize, embrace, and triumph time and again with the novel concept of railroads martial, the Second Reich used them as well on the huge tracts of the Dark Continent in a bid to eventually conquer all of it, but failed. This was detailed in the 1915 Norton *Report:*

> Aided by the strategic railways already built in Southwest Africa, German troops were to join the Boer rising when *Der Tag* arrived—and was confidently expected—in acquiring possession of British Southwest Africa. The German East African Railway—connecting the Indian Ocean with the shores of Lake Tanganyika—was to enable German troops to make raids into British East Africa; to secure the eventual supremacy of Germany in the Belgian Congo with its vast potentialities in the way of mineral and other resources; and to join with German troops coming via the northeast corner of German Southwest Africa in the seizure of Rhodesia. Then—as originally designed—the northern railway of the German Cameroons was to be continued to Lake Chad, whence, it was hoped, Germany would get control over the Sudan and over the French

possessions in North Africa, linking up Lake Chad with Algeria and the Mediterranean by what would then be a German railway across the Sahara Desert.

The line upon which this overly ambitious plan was based, though, was never able, added the Norton *Report:*

> To bring the trade and traffic of the Belgian Congo under the direction of Germany, by securing it either for the German East African Railway or for the new German lines connecting the Congo with the chief port of the Cameroons, for a coastal railway connection between German Southwest Africa and Portuguese Angola (helping to ensure the ultimate possession thereof for Germany); and for the extension of the Lobito Bay Railway to the southern districts of the Belgian Congo as part of a German line of rail communication from the west coast across Central Africa to the east, had all failed of realization at the time that war broke out; though here we get further evidence of the nature of the aims that Germany was cherishing.

Suppose the Germans had won outright their African war, and in the Middle East, the Turks had not been beaten by the Allies? What a dual railway line linkup victory that might have been! This would have resulted overall in not only all of the African Continent as a major part of the new German World Reich, but German railroads as well, stretching out from Hamburg to Istanbul, the Persian Gulf, Cairo, and the Cape.

The first setback to any such grandiose scheme of global conquest came with the flop of the Boer uprising that never was, joined with the conquest of GSWA by Gen. Louis Botha's army, conversely. The British Army seized outright that colony's expensive (8 million Reich Marks) SWA Railways, deploying on it British Empire troops instead. These were linked to those of the British South African Union, thereafter helping to administer the former GSWA colony under Britain's own Cape Province government. Nairobi, Kenya-backed British Army commanding officer Brig-Gen. M. I. Tighe's train suffered ambush *en route*, the line itself destroyed by explosives. Bullets blasted into the general's own command coach during the nighttime attack with rifles. Enraged, the general himself ran toward the flashes in the darkness, swearing profusely and waving his swagger stick in anger.

Firing back from the train with what was its sole rifle, Capt. R. Meinertzhagen failed to stop the German night raiders' escape into the bush to fight another day. The resultant railway precautions and rail traffic slowed to but 15 mph, with all locomotives guarded by forward trucks of sand.

Enter the Kaiser's East African "Lawrence:"
Gen. Paul von Lettow-Vorbeck

The famous German colonial army commander Col. Paul Emil von Lettow-Vorbeck (1870–1964), whose principal pre-First World War campaigns were the Boxer Rebellion in China of 1900–01, and the Hottentot-Herero Rebellion of 1904–08—now coming under harsh scrutiny as "the Kaiser's Holocaust" of these exterminated natives—and of 1914–18 in East Africa. Lettow cannily had his men set explosive detonation times to go off only after a desired number of wheels had already crossed over. When this ingenious tactic was discovered, the British countered by placing its vital engines at the rear of even more protective railway trucks.

Lettow Foiled by Meinertzhagen

On 24 August 1915, a German sabotage patrol was captured, and prevented from the planned demolition of the Tsavo Bridge. Capt. R. Meinertzhagen took prisoner an educated Arab who was his German service rival sabotaging the Uganda Railway, and had him shot. Throughout the campaign of 1915, von Lettow did his utmost to destroy Britain's Ugandan Railway, but he was handicapped in having insufficient facilities for the transport of his men and materials as there were only two lines in his territory.

The Lunatic Express/Lettow's Unconquered Nemesis:
Britain's Uganda Railway

This was so-termed because of its many difficulties and unfortunate happenings occasioned by its construction. In 1884, the as-yet unclaimed Uganda in East Africa lay between British Kenya and the German East African colony that encompassed Burundi, Rwanda, and Tanganyika. The British announced their projected Uganda Railway starting on Kenya's coast to Lake Victoria in the interior near the Ugandan frontier, with actual building commencing in 1896 with 32,000 workers. Reportedly, the work alone killed 2,498, but the line was finished in 1901. When the Great War broke out, it was not at first certain that the conflict would carry over into colonial Africa. As the news arrived and then spread, though, the white colonialists themselves brought the war to the Dark Continent by volunteering to fight. At Nairobi's railroad station platform, a demonstration occurred complete with placards urging enlistment in the local British colonial home defense units. The result was the establishment of the British Kenyan East African Mounted Rifles to patrol the southern border with the now enemy German East Africa, and also to protect the at once vulnerable Uganda Railway.

Von Lettow's Guerilla War against the Uganda Railway

During 12 April–10 May 1916 there were 57 more German attempts to destroy the Uganda Railway via sabotage, but all failed. To join the Central Railway to that of the Usambara, a connecting track was laid, and over it 8,000 carriers rode, divided into sizable groupings that transited the region by portions. The Germans constructed railroad bridges, and one of concrete and stone. Lettow's attacks on the Uganda Railway helped prevent a British invasion of the imperiled German East Africa temporarily.

In his postwar memoirs, Lettow recalled, "With the greatest energy, we continued our enterprises against the Uganda Railway into 1916." Another of his main Allied opponents was the well-known former Boer Army leader, and later British Army Field Marshal Jan Smuts, who hoped to bring Lettow's smaller force to battle by pushing on down the Uganda Railway, building a line southward to Taveta. This outstanding engineering feat was accomplished in truly daunting conditions, its final leg finished in one 10-day burst of building. According to one dispatch:

> In all, 10½ miles of line were laid—including initial surveying and digging—plus plate laying, and the construction of a triple-span bridge … The advance on Kahe began on 18 March….

Smut's engineers built a line connecting the Uganda Railway to the Usambara Railway, and on 25 April, the first train from Vol—on the Uganda Railway —steamed into Moshi, there being as yet no Mwanza-Tabora railroad. The hardy British colonials also built 11 new Uganda Railway stations on the Samburu-Kui line, as well as improving maintenance of the overall Uganda Railway. Starting in February 1915, another line was built—Voi-Maktau-Kahe—the latter already a Tanga-Moshi line station. This was mainly a military railway to transit troops and supplies, built by 1,500 African and 300 Indian laborers.

The Indian stationmaster at Tsavo sent an unintentionally hilarious telegram text for help that read: "100 Germans advancing on the station; please send one rifle and 100 rounds of ammunition." Yet another such Indian witticism resulted from this defining the difference between

His Majesty's Armoured Train *Simba.* This was built in the British Nairobi railway workshop in ten days.

a collision and an explosion: "A collision, there you are; an explosion, where are you?"

The British Nairobi Railway workshop produced HMAT, the acronym for His Majesty's Armored Train, *Simba* in just 10 working days to be deployed as a railway line protector versus would-be German saboteurs. Wartime stations featured steam-up replacement plus repair trains for speedy deployment as required, keeping the lines operable versus the always persistent German railroad raiding parties. Nocturnal railway travel for freight was shut down for almost a year, greatly halting valuable trading.

Great Britain versus German East Africa

The capital of German East Africa was at the seacoast port town of Dar-es-Salaam. In July 1914, there had just been completed the last leg of the westward running Ujiji–Lake Tanganyika Railway, following trying months of tough engineering problems and natural difficulties overcome. The war came as a shock to Germany's top colonial commander in German East Africa, then Col. von Lettow-Vorbeck. From its outset, his main strategic dilemma was that his two major railroads—the Moshi–Tanganyika Central and Usambara Railways—lacked linkage together. To alleviate this, Lettow with a thousand of his best troops set off on the Uganda Railway at top speed with his black *askari* [native] troops riding in the hot sun onward to the sea via rocky gorges that would have made excellent spots for enemy ambuscades. His goal was Moshi, the region's largest and most German township, heading the Uganda Railway at one end. Their main task was to outrun the region's seasonal monsoon downpours via surrounding foothills and jungles. Along with the British, Lettow also had a Belgian Army opponent, Gen. Tombeur, who advanced south to the German Central Railway's west end, leading the Germans to retreat, rather than fight a pitched battle that it might not win. Meanwhile, British then-Lt-Gen. Smuts was also moving against this Central line in two parries. If he could seize the Central Railway intact, Smuts' Empire forces would have under its sway most of the German colony's landmass that included its ports, inland towns, and communication lines. Smuts sent one column south to the railway itself, with him leading the main force on the Uganda Railway, departing it later to the Central Railway in line with his Allied van Deventer force. Smuts believed that he had hoodwinked the wily Lettow into feeling that the entire Allied force was moving on the Uganda Railway alone, but in this he was proven wrong.

Although Lettow had strongly reinforced the local German garrison on the Uganda Railway, he now withdrew it, sparing these troops defeat by the larger Allied force. Smuts launched his drive on the Uganda Railway on 22 May 1916, planning to halt at Tanga, then veer southward aligned with his detached van Deventer units some 150 miles distant and eastward, striking toward the Handeni road juncture. For the British, their further advance starting from the railway would be opposed by about 3,000 enemy German forces. As usual, Lettow withdrew, while Smuts struck south for the Uganda Railway, prior to taking the port of Tanga, which remained German. Lettow's overall 6,000-strong forces successfully harassed the Smuts expedition of 45,000 Allied soldiers, a remarkable military achievement. Forced by the war's loss in Europe to stand down at last with his own, separate, and never defeated African command, back home in the Reich, von Lettow-Vorbeck was considered a martial hero. Lettow in 1919 returned to Berlin in the Reich's sole postwar victory parade of the entire Great War experience, even after all European theaters had already been lost to the enemy. How had he done it?

In 1914, Lettow told his civilian superior—Colonial Gov. Dr Heinrich Schnee:

> British East Africa shares a frontier with us. Just beyond it is the Uganda Railway. If we cut it, we cut Britain's supply line from the ocean at Mombasa to Nairobi and the interior—and that Britain cannot afford to have happen. She will react.

Later, he told a subordinate:

The destruction of the Uganda Railway and telegraph lines along it should begin at once. Fast work and surprise attacks will have the best results. Off you go! Take the initiative. Wipe out the British on the frontier!

This feisty colonial soldier of the faraway Second Reich in Central Europe, "Could continue to sting the British by his fighting patrols along the Uganda Railway." His British foe Meinertzhagen's patrols uprooted the German encampments that had been established in the vicinity of the Uganda Railway, and drove them back across their own frontiers, short of water and ammunition, retired.

During the spring and summer of 1915, Lettow's main target remained the British Uganda Railway that carried supplies to Nairobi and its farther reaches from Port Mombasa and the sea beyond. Lettow wisely broke down his own far outnumbered native colonial forces into bands of eight black *askaris* with two white officers each to raid, plunder, and destroy behind British lines. Hiding in the wooded slopes along towering Mt Kilimanjaro, they hit time and again both the Uganda and Magad Railways, taking bored sentries by surprise, burning bridges, mining the lines, and in general raiding all ground communications running between the railroads and the enemy's own encampments. Knowing also that the British were constructing a line from the Uganda Railway's Vol station to the frontier post of Maktau looking toward Mt Kilimanjaro, Lettow wrote:

> The construction of this military line proved that an attack with large forces was in preparation, and that it was to be directed against this part of the Kilimanjaro country.

By 1 January 1916, the British railway and water pipeline from Vol was almost finished to Salaita, but could go no further with its German-native foe still safe on the slopes above them. Gov. Schnee was by now full of praise for von Lettow's black troops, especially impressed as he was by their frequent mining of the Uganda Railway.

His main Great War battles were in his famed East African campaign: Tanga in Tanzania in 1914, and Mahiwa there in 1917. He was considered by two period authorities as:

> One of the most successful and … most gifted guerilla leaders of all time … With never more than 12,000 men, he tied down 10–20 times as many British and other Allied troops. Only the official end of the war brought him—still unvanquished—to surrender.

Celebrated back at Berlin, his long military career came to an abrupt end with his participation in the failed anti-government Kapp *putsch* to restore the ex-Kaiser to his throne, put down by the peacetime army. Lettow died at Hamburg on 9 March 1964, aged 96.

The Berlin–Baghdad Railway at War, 1914–18

German Württemburg United Banker and arms salesman Alfred vom Kaulla and German Bank managing director Georg von Siemens jointly established a syndicate, to which Turkey granted the concession whereby the then current Haydarpasa–Ismit Railway would connect with the Turks' capital of Ankara, thereby birthing the new Anatolian Railway Company, finished in December 1892. With working stations established at Eskisehir, the German railway moguls pushed on to the Konya, with this additional line finished in July 1896, they then becoming the first and second Baghdad-to-Berlin/Berlin to Baghdad Railway sections. By 1914, the future anti-Reich trio of Allies recognized that any successful Berlin to Baghdad Railway could—and probably would—bring Berlin into better contact with her then colonial empire of German East Africa and also German Southwest Africa, and also further cement a dawning Reich-Turkish military pact. They need not have worried, though, as—right from the start—the Berlin to Baghdad Railway faced all manner of obstacles political and geographical. Still, the day after the Great War commenced on 1 August 1914, a top-secret Ottoman Empire-Second Reich alliance was, in fact, signed. Nonetheless, the British Army in Mesopotamia—and the pre-war and wartime denial of passage to the Persian Gulf—kept Wilhelm II out of the area.

The complicated lines featured a yawning gap of 300 miles separating them, plus a trio of mountains through which the Berlin to Baghdad Railway would tunnel—"someday." This meant that—at war's outset—the Berlin to Baghdad Railway was in reality four separate railroad segments, making the journey by rail via Istanbul-Baghdad a full 22 days across a distance of 1,255 miles in all. These breaks in service seriously hampered the Ottoman Army in supporting its Mesopotamian provincial battlefronts, isolating both it and them from all the other Turkish Army units' widely scattered combat regions. With limited funds and manpower, the Germans and Turks continued building, though, but with only two of the four gaps being closed.

It was during the four years of the Great War that oil fully emerged as a—if not the—key to winning modern wars, based on gasoline fuel and oil lubrication of motor-driven vehicles of all kinds. Afterwards, it

Paul Emil von Lettow-Vorbeck (1870–1964) (center) was a general in the Imperial German Army and the commander of its forces in the German East Africa campaign. For four years, with a force that never exceeded about 14,000 (3,000 Germans and 11,000 Africans), he held in check a much larger force of 300,000 British, Belgian, and Portuguese troops. He is seen here centre, early 1919, with a British officer to his right side.

Essentially undefeated in the field, Lettow-Vorbeck was the only German commander to successfully invade imperial British soil during the First World War. In March 1919 he paraded in Pariser Platz, Berlin and was given a hero's welcome. *Bundesarchiv*

Turkish flags fly from a station on the Hejaz Railway.

A locomotive and train at the station in Ma'an on the Hejaz Railway.

A tempting target on the Hejaz Railway.

was estimated that World War I caused 16-20 million deaths, of which 10 million or more were civilians, oil helping to cause these losses. Indeed, one expert has written, "The Allies were carried to victory on a flood of oil." In May 1916, the two western Allied powers signed the Sykes-Picot Agreement named after two civil servants, the first British and the second French. By its top-secret terms, Great Britain was promised post-war rights to build a railway from Haifa to Baghdad via the French post-war Zone of Occupation of Syria and Lebanon.

In 1914, the Berlin to Baghdad Railway consisted of the already built and world famous *Orient Express,* plus the newer line of Constantinople [Istanbul]–Baghdad, that ran via Turkey, Syria, and Iraq. The main, immediate German aim was to gain a seaport on the Persian Gulf, while the Ottomans viewed the Berlin to Baghdad Railway as another means of keeping in place their vast Arabian province, even though it was considered the least important of many.

The Ottoman Empire also sought to establish a bridgehead of influence in British Egypt—that had once belonged to it—over the Red Sea. Not surprisingly, therefore, the Berlin to Baghdad Railway became a pre-war focal point of intense international tension between the Second Reich and the future wartime Allies. Some have regretted that—by 1914—all the relevant bones of contention among the Great Powers were already resolved, even prior to the war's outbreak. By 1915—with the war in full swing—the Berlin to Baghdad Railway remained 300 miles lacking completion, thereby making it almost useless for the waging of First World

War militarily. Still, the Allies fretted over what might occur if and when the Berlin to Baghdad Railway came online during the war. Connected to the future Basra Railway, the Berlin to Baghdad Railway would mean full transport and commercial trade from the Second Reich—via its new Persian Gulf port—to the Empire's far-flung colonies in both Africa and the Pacific. This was despite the fact that the British had already taken the former and the Japanese the latter, but the rest of the world still beckoned.

Coming back to the Reich—the Allies dreaded—would also be a direct oil supply to help fuel German heavy industry. The Tsar viewed Russia as imperiled by the Berlin to Baghdad Railway, as it would bring the Reich foreign office to its own Caucasian border, and on to north Persia, both of which the Russians considered their own economic domain, as in centuries past. Simultaneously, German railroad engineers built the Hejaz Railway in Arabia later made famous by British Army Maj. T. E. Lawrence, during 1916–18 as he blew up various segments of it for Britain and her "Arab friends." The famed Hejaz had been built as the pet project of Turkish Sultan Abdul Hamid II. The Hejaz was wisely placed outside the range of British Royal Navy gunnery, with the Iskenderub–Alleppo seaside kept bare of tracks. Instead, the Hejaz traversed the Amanus Mountain range with costly engineering that encompassed the 8 km Ayran–Fevzipasa Tunnel, but did not link the Ottoman Empire directly to the Second Reich.

In 1915, the Berlin to Baghdad Railway extended 50 miles east of Dijarbakir, with a second spur offshoot concluded at Nusaybin, east of Aleppo. More tracks snaked there way north to Tirkit to Baghdad, and on south to Kut.

Turkey's Embattled Hejaz Railway in Arabia, 1908–20

Overall, the Ottoman Empire's road and highway system was never more than adequate, while in the vast Arabian Hejaz Desert, there was effectively none at all. Only the native Bedouins traveled overland, by camel. Most travel for non-natives was by sea or train, being subject to pirates on water and brigands on land. Duly proposed but incomplete were a pair of train routes: the Berlin to Baghdad Railway and the Istanbul–Medina line, otherwise and popularly known as the Hejaz Railway. Conceived in 1864, the Hejaz Railway's chief engineer Mouktar Bey started from Damascus and arrived at its end point of Medina with its completion—debt-free—on 1 September 1908, in honor of the Turkish sultan's accession to the throne. The ornate Damascus Station opened in 1913, with several miles of the Hejaz Railway's tracks ran below sea level. One humorous anecdote noted that: "Due to the locals' habit of pulling up wooden sleepers to fuel

T. E. (Thomas Edward) Lawrence (1888–1935) was an author, archaeologist, military officer, and diplomat. He was renowned for his liaison role during the Sinai and Palestine Campaign and the Arab Revolt against the Ottoman Empire during the First World War.

Arab irregulars fighting with T. E. Lawrence in the Sinai, 1917.

Field Marshal August von Mackensen (center, in spiked helmet) inspects a Turkish guard of honor at Sfirkedji Station at Constantinople [Istanbul] on 24 March 1915. Note also the Turkish Army officers at left wearing fez. *Library of Congress*

German Army soldiers ride the Baghdad Railway near the end of the Great War in 1918. *Library of Congress*

their campfires, some sections of the track were laid on iron sleepers." To augment the Hejaz Railway, Turkish military engineers constructed an offshoot line to Beersheba that opened on 30 October 1915, after the first full year of the Great War.

Due to a gauge change from 1.44 to 1.05 meters at Rayak, the Hejaz broke down into a pair of separate lines, and troop shipments from Turkey found themselves water-bound between the two disconnected sections. This was where British naval power came into play, meaning that the Turkish Army was unable to use the Suez Canal, Hejaz then being the main means of fast bulk traffic. Even *The Handbook of the Turkish Army* described the Hejaz Railway as a branch offshoot line of the larger Rayak–Damascus–Deraa–Beersheba Railway. It is ironic that the partial author of this work was Lt Thomas Edward Lawrence (of Arabia)! The Hejaz Railway had too many technical disadvantages: narrow gauge and single track, a roadbed poorly and cheaply built. Its limited capacity also suffered by having sufficient water for only one train daily, while lack of fuel gave way to firing cotton waste, reducing power necessary for pullage. The Turkish Army's isolated Medina garrison was dependent entirely on a Hejaz Railway that was easily disrupted by enemy saboteurs, with an ever increasing number of soldiers forced to protect it. This reduced the garrison's ability to combat the Allied armies opposite them. The Arabian part of the Turkish Army comprised the following reported units:

> Ottoman 1st Composite Force—3,000 strong—was based on Maan, and operated southward. 2nd Composite Force (5,000 men) was based on Tebuk, about 300 miles north of Medina … 8,000 troops to guard the lines of communication for 16,000, mainly contained in the Medina area.

The 800-mile-long Hejaz Railway Damascus–Medina Railway was interspersed with 79 stations guarded by Turkish Army-manned two-three blockhouses at each station that formed small desert forts for every 10 miles. These were in visual sight of one another up and down the line, and thereby able to send each other aid as required. In between these small "forts," were placed smaller "fortlets," plus hilltop trenches that overlooked each and all. There were deployed 1–300 men at each of the forts, with either infantry squads or platoons along the entire 800 miles of desert. In theory—and sometimes even in actual practice—this "one-dimensional line from start to finish" was a workable stratagem. However, as noted by Faulkner, "The desert was not like this, but an infinity of points with two dimensions."

Under the inspired hit-and-run guerilla war leadership of T. E. Lawrence the Allies' "Arabs" of various nomadic tribesmen attacked the far more numerous and better armed Turks in small raiding groups backed by British artillery, planes, and armored cars where possible, in a very efficient desert war. Compared to the vast amounts of money, troops, and railway repairs necessitated to guard against Lawrence's raiders, the Arab War was cheaper and more successful than that waged in Arabia by the Turks. After his initial first raid of 19 September 1917, 30 others were made on trains and not trackage, as the Turkish Army repaired that. Still, the latter's rail traffic was reduced from two a day to but a pair a week. Another important raid was on 6 October 1917 at the mined Shedia Bridge that destroyed a 12-car train with 20 Turks killed and the rest taken prisoner, including four officers. An estimated 70 tons of food was loaded onto camels in less than an hour afterwards. However, the train was not burned in time, as 40 would-be Turkish Army rescuers were but 40 yards' distant when Lawrence and his band made good their escape without any casualties whatever.

Here is Lawrence himself describing some of his operations in his postwar memoirs of 1926:

> Our capture of [the Turk's Arabian port of] Aqaba closed the Hejaz War, and gave us the task of helping the British invade Syria … We organized the Aqaba area as an unassailable base from which to hinder the Hejaz Railway … The death of a Turkish bridge or rail … was more profitable to us than the death of a Turk … In railway cutting, it would be usually an empty stretch of rail, and the more empty, the greater the tactical success.

Thus, it was Lawrence's tactical practice to:

> Develop a habit of never engaging the enemy … Many Turks on our front had no chance all the war to fire on us, and we were never on the defensive, except by accident and in error …

In order to set up his successful ambushes of trains and destruction of bridges along which they ran:

> We climbed a sand peak to spy out the railway … We worked fast, and did great damage [with set mines and planted charges of explosives. On one such operation alone] We ruined 10 bridges and many rails.

Another hallmark of his raids was flexibility in adapting them to rapidly changing circumstances:

A damaged viaduct on the Hejaz Railway.

A water tank in Daraa, Syria, on the Hejaz Railway.

Maan was impregnable for us, so we concentrated on cutting its northern railway and diverting the Turkish effort to relieve its garrison from the Amman side.

On 19 September 1917:

I rushed uphill, and saw by its shape and volume that, indeed, there must be a train waiting in the station … Suddenly, it moved out in our direction. We yelled to the Arabs to get into position … The men with rifles posted themselves in a long line behind the spur … From it, they would fire directly into the derailed carriages at less than 150 yards, whereas the ranges for the Stokes and Lewis guns were about 300 yards. An Arab stood up on high behind the guns and shouted to us what the train was doing—a necessary precaution—for if it carried troops and detrained them behind our ridge, we should have to face about like a flash and retire fighting up the valley for our lives. Fortunately, it held on at all the speed the two locomotives could make on wood fuel … The engines—looking very big—rocked with screaming whistles into view around the bend. Behind them followed 10 boxcars, crowded with rifle muzzles at the windows and doors, and in little sandbag nests on the roofs, Turks precariously held on, to shoot at us. I had not thought of two engines, and on the moment decided to fire the charge under the second, so that however little the mine's effect, the uninjured engine should not be able to uncouple and drag the carriages away…. When the front 'driver' of the second engine was on the bridge, I raised my hand … There followed a terrific roar, and the line vanished from sight behind a spouting column of black dust and smoke 100 feet high and wide. Out of the darkness came shattering crashes and long, loud metallic clangings of ripped steel, with many lumps of iron and plate, while one entire wheel of a locomotive whirled up suddenly black out of the cloud against the sky, and sailed musically over our heads to fall slowly and heavily into the desert behind. Except for the flight of these, there succeeded a deathly silence—with no cry of men or rifle shot— as the now grey mist of the explosion drifted from the line towards us, and over our ridge until it was lost in the hills … I looked around to see what was happening so quickly, and saw the train stationary and dismembered along the track, with its wagon sides jumping under the bullets that riddled them, while Turks were falling out from the far doors to gain the shelter of the railway embankment. As I watched, our machineguns chattered out over my head, and the long rows of Turks on the carriage roofs rolled over, and were swept off the top like bales of cotton before the furious shower of bullets that stormed along the roofs and splashed clouds of yellow chips from the planking … The remaining Turks had got behind the bank … and from the cover of the wheels were firing … but Stokes slipped in the first shell … and there came a crash as it burst beyond the train in the desert … His second shot fell just by the trucks in the deep hollow below the bridge where the Turks were taking refuge—it made a shambles of the place. The survivors … broke out in a panic across the desert, throwing away their rifles and equipment as they ran. This was the opportunity of the Lewis gunners. The sergeant grimly traversed with drum after drum, till the open sand was littered with bodies … the battle over … the others [Arabs] were beginning … to tear open the carriages and fall to plunder. It had taken nearly 10 minutes … Succeeding wagons were derailed and smashed, some had frames irreparably buckled. The second engine was a blanched pile of smoking iron. Its driving wheels had been blown upward, taking away the side of the firebox. Cab and tender were twisted into strips, among the piled stones of the abutment. It would never run again. The front engine had got off better: though heavily derailed and lying half over— with the cab burst—yet its steam was at pressure, and driving gear intact. Our greatest object was to destroy locomotives … The Turks later found the engine beyond use, and broke it up.

Statistically from this single action, the Turks lost 70 men killed, mainly from the Stokes mortar and the Lewis machine gun fire, plus 30 POWs and three wounded, as opposed to but a pair of Arabs killed and a trio wounded. The train was pillaged with the raiders fleeing on their camels as a Turkish relief column—having spied the battle from afar—was closing in on Lawrence to support their compatriots, but were too late.

The Turks were quick to respond, too, where, when, how, and as best they could:

There came a loud boom from the railway, and a shell shattered among our sleeping host. The Turks had sent down an armored train mounting a field gun …

The Hejaz Railway War was the last in which the sturdy Arabian camel played a key role in winning a major victory, for the desert was the domain of the camel, and not of the mechanical train, whose working parts lubricated by oil were often foiled by the gritty sand of the desert wastes. In this two dimensional war of the "Ship of the Desert" versus the single path Iron Horse, the camel was both ideally suited and thus destined to win, and did. The camel could move in all dimensions, whereas the static train was chained to its rails. Lawrence saw immediately that

Auda ibu Tayi
(*c.* 1874–1924), second from right, was the leader of a section of the Howeitat or Huwaytat tribe of Bedouin Arabs at the time of the Great Arab Revolt during the First World War. Lawrence recorded that the Howeitat had formerly been under the leadership of the House of Rashid, the amirs of Ha'il, but had since fragmented and that Auda had come to control the eastern section, the abu Tayi. Tensions between them and the Ottoman administration had increased after an incident in 1908, when two soldiers were killed who had been sent to demand payment of a tax that Auda claimed to have already paid.

Mounted Arab tribesmen. T. E. Lawrence gathered a formidable force of Arabs in his campaign against the Hejaz Railway.

desert warfare was more like a war at sea than one on land, and waged it as such. Faulkner later wrote:

> Against an insurgency that was everywhere and nowhere, to defend the railway line at all was to defend the whole of it. Thus might 100 men tie down 1,000—even 10,000—and every station Damascus to Medina was thus equally threatened at all times.

The Arab Revolt based at Aqaba was supplied from the sea by the Royal Navy, being able to strike all along the Hejaz Railway. Indeed, this was the how and the why of Lawrence's successful strategy.

During July to September 1917, 30 bridges and 10,000 rails were torn up along the Maan–Medina railway segment, it being attacked on the average of once every three days. In October 1917, fully 2,000 Bedouins in three separate attacks on a 75-mile-long stretch of rails south of Hallat–Amman saw trains derailed with 250 Turks either killed or taken prisoner, and a hilltop redoubt of 180 men also being taken and held by the Arabs themselves for four days. Statistically for the last four months of 1917, 17 engines and "scores of wagons" were destroyed in railway raids on the Turkish right flank that caused the Turks to reinforce, "100 tiny posts." During the Maan Railway "siege" campaign, Lawrence told his superior Gen. Sir Edmund Allenby that his strategy was not to break the line, but rather to keep it just in working order instead to Medina so that the Turkish Army would continue to defend it by sending out more men. Breaking the line would make of Maan a railhead, for which his Bedouins were ill suited to take. Wrecking trains was the ideal usage of his fast-moving, lightly armed, highly mobile guerillas instead.

For the November 1917 Deraa–Damascus campaign, Gen. Allenby wanted now Col. Lawrence to mount an operation deep into the Turks' rear at the railway town of Deraa, 60 miles south of Damascus where the Palestine line branched off the main Hejaz Line. If Deraa was taken, the entire Palestinian rail network with connections to Haifa, Jaffa, Jerusalem, Gaza, and Beersheba would be cut off, as Damascus was the navel of the Turkish Army in Syria, the command point of all their fronts. Due to the weather that late in the annual campaigning season, Lawrence suggested instead the blowing up of a large bridge of the Yarmuk Railway that would also close down communications on the same Palestinian front, and the general agreed with this counter operation, scheduled for 5 November 1917. The raid had to be aborted, however, so Lawrence planned an alternate one for the 7th. Two complete trains passed Lawrence as he was himself exposed to the view of the Turkish soldiers aboard before he was ready to strike on 11 November 1917. A train of two engines and

T. E. Lawrence's exploits were much publicized. He died in a motor cycle accident in 1935.

12 coaches was exploded, on which was an Ottoman general officer, but then 200 Turks lined an embankment to fight 60 Arab riflemen without machine guns; 40 Turks charged, but were repulsed. Lawrence and his men escaped, but they had been defeated nonetheless.

Without enough money to pay Arab tribal brigands, the Yarmuk raid also suffered via lack of native enthusiasm. Lawrence was caught by a Turkish patrol at Deraa, suspected of being a light skinned deserter from either army, and allegedly raped by the town's Turkish Army garrison commander. He considered himself spent as a fighting force, asked to be sent home, and was granted his request by Gen. Allenby. This was not before Lawrence, the Arab Prince Faisal, and the general all triumphed over the Turks, however: "The united forces entered Damascus unopposed." In sum, it was a remarkable victory.

After the war in the United Kingdom, American newspaper reporter and savvy media promoter Lowell Thomas created the romantic legend of *Lawrence of Arabia* that continues to resonate still, and that transcended the mud and blood of the Western Front trench war in Europe. Without the Turkish Hejaz Railway, however, none of it would ever have happened. Tragically, Col. Lawrence died in a motorbike accident in 1935.

Hospital Trains

During the 1870–71 war, the Germans had 21 "vestibuled" hospital trains that treated its 90,000 wounded. Perhaps not too surprisingly, the Great War commenced with no major power having any real plan for the care of its expected wounded casualties, nor did the overall situation improve much by war's end in November 1918. Both sides never solved, either, their chronic dilemma of unreturned railway freight cars, another persistent problem carried forward from 1859–71. In addition, fatal accidental crashes increased, three of them major in scope.

Russia: Germany's Railway Opponent

In 1837, the very first town in the vast Tsarist Empire to receive railway traffic was at *Tsarskoye Selo* [The Tsar's Village], joined at His Majesty's summer capital of St Petersburg 15 miles away. The Tsarskoye Selo line had its own railway platform with ornate station featuring a high, pitched roof, the line running astride a lengthy boulevard to the Imperial Park's gateway. Thus, the Tsar—like his cousin the Kaiser at Wildpark, Potsdam—had his own, personal train station. The Russian winters at St Petersburg were so bitter cold that its Neva River and canal system froze over solid, with, huge sheets of thick blue ice. This allowed for tram tracks to actually be laid over the river's surface.

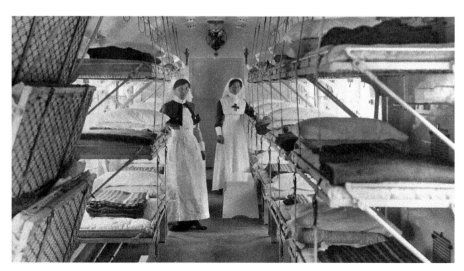

A Great Western Railway hospital train.

A German hospital train with space to load a horizontal stretcher before being carried into the carriage bunk.

The Danish-born mother of the Tsar—the Dowager Empress Marie Feodorovna—maintained a traveling retinue of 200 on her special train. Dumbfounded by all this railway opulence, Russian onlookers stood gawking in awe at trackside. At Tsarskoye Selo, the young and very ill Heir to the throne Tsarevich Alexis had his own toy train set. Indeed it was described by one palace authority as:

> Great railways—with dolls in the carriages as passengers—with barriers, stations, buildings, and signal boxes, flashing engines, and marvelous signaling apparatus ... All the toys were mechanically worked, and the little prince had only to press a button to set the workers in motion....

Writing in 1884 during then Prince Wilhelm of Prussia's second rail trip to Tsarist Russia, Court Marshal Eduard von Liebenau stated that the railway lines on which Tsar Alexander III, "Intended to travel were patrolled b ... 12,000 soldiers." That same year, the Trans-Asia Railway began construction, to run 9,300 miles.

German Army Deputy Chief of General Staff Gen. Count Alfred von Waldersee recorded in his diary in spring 1886:

While it may be true that the Emperor Alexander does not want to go to war with us, Russia is nonetheless strongly suspicious of us ... It is also characteristic that (Russian) preparations for war—and especially the expansion of the railway system for military purposes—have gone on unabated for years.

Conversely, in 1892, Kaiser Wilhelm II wrote to his grandmother Queen Victoria on Russian railroads:

The whole of the transport system on the lines have been utterly muddled, so that a lot of engines and wagons have up to the number of 500 and 14,000 respectively been broken down or spoiled by snowdrifts ... they are beyond hope of repair.

The Tsar's Railway Regiment and Imperial Train Travel

His Majesty's Russian Army Railway Regiment had two battalions of a thousand soldiers, with Vladimir Voyekov administering it, and Gen. Labl in actual command martial. Both were held responsible for all Imperial train travel across the vast empire. Prior to departures, the entire train was inspected to prevent accidents or attacks by terrorists. Once the trip started, Gen. Labl was aboard in charge of security. In 1888, there occurred the family accident during which two tsars were present; present and future. That October, the Imperial train derailed near Kharkov as the family dined. Using his famous physical strength, Tsar Alexander III held up the collapsed dining car ceiling as his family crawled out to safety unscathed. Over-the-top and far too opulent rail travel was all the rage at the Russian Court, with Nicholas II's uncle/brother-in-law Grand Duke Sergei Alexandrovich purchasing his own railway saloon car merely to travel but 18 miles total from Moscow to Ilinskoye, his country *dacha*. The sumptuously furnished, personal coach of this Governor General of Moscow boasted bedroom, bath, anteroom and drawing room lounge, plus costly interior décor and upholstery at £3,500 pounds Sterling, all billed to the Moscow–Brest Railway Company. Due to its excessive weight, however, it saw only 10 years' actual service.

As with his more flamboyant cousin Wilhelm II, Tsar Nicholas II also had a luxurious Imperial train of 10 cars cast in deep blue exterior paint and crested with gold twin-headed eagles. Fully 1,000 feet long, the Imperial rail conveyance was constructed during 1894–96 at the Alexandrovsky Mechanical Works from plans used in 1892 for that made for Tsar Alexander III. The individual cars were built at several sites both

Above and below : The Russian imperial train crash of 1888.

within and without the empire, including Paris, Berlin, and even Warsaw, the latter then a Tsarist subject city. Interior fittings hailed from both Austria and Finland, the latter part of the Tsar's far-reaching domains of that era. These included within the coaches a variety of exquisite wooden furnishings: oak, beech, maple, teak, walnut, red beech, satin wood, and Karelian birch; the floors carpeted with rugs and linoleum tile. Walls were festooned by silk, leather, and floral British cretonne; plus wooden panels inlaid with beech, mother-of-pearl, satinwood, and tortoiseshell. The train's last coach had its power station for internal electric appliances, telephones, and air-conditioning for all travel compartments.

Subsequent upgraded safety features included dual brake controls—Hardy air discharge and Westinghouse compressed air brakes—and had a third emergency set, just in case the prior two did not halt the Imperial coaches as required. The Imperial Escort rode in the train's initial coach and included both Palace Protection Squad troopers as well as railway battalion officers. A kitchen, wine room, and pantry—plus living quarters for chef, butler, wine steward, and galley staff—were in the second car. The third car's anteroom gave way to the dining area, with mahogany panels offset by brocaded silk. Curtains of satin and blue-green velvet were suspended from the windows' carved pediments. The ornate, white-paneled ceiling had inset tiny crystal fixtures and frosted glass-globed ormolu chandeliers. The car sat 16 diners, comfortably in brown leather covered chairs at an oaken table. The Tsar generally took his place at mid-table, his son and daughters to the Imperial sides. Oddly, his rather strange consort Empress Alexandra ate alone in her boudoir. The fourth car was the mobile drawing room, its walls draped in damask of colored olive between moldings of mahogany wood. The chairs and sofas were also made of mahogany, with green stripes and cream silk coverlets, while overhead light shown down via silk-shaded ormolu, art nouveau pattern lamps, sconces, and chandeliers.

An upright piano graced a corner, on a green rug woven in a pattern of trellised flowers. The fifth coach contained the personal quarters of the Imperial couple. The monarch's office had a dark leather, built-in couch sitting among Karelian birch wooden bookcases; his desk sited between a pair of windows, with an elaborate pen fixture, Fabergé paper knives and a silver ashtray. Draped with black silk, the Imperial couple's sleeping area had a pair of brass beds under iconic clusters, the connecting bath featuring a copper-lined sunken tub engineered in a corner with ledges, to prevent water spillage as the train kept rolling onward across the steppes. Her Majesty's ornate boudoir had cedar and Karelian birch furnishings, plus walls covered in silk and mauve. Next came her small drawing room, plus living areas for his valet and her maid. The Imperial children's rooms

The imperial train.

The private study and sleeping-car of Emperor Nicholas II.

A salon carriage on the
imperial train.

and living quarters for Alexandra's suite were in the next car, with two
following for luggage and personal staff. As both Their Majesties were
highly religious, shortly after the train's "completion," there was added
a chapel coach with Russian icons with a belfry, its bell chiming as the
assemblage sped across country.

The Imperial train was staffed by 26 people: four each of valets, cooks,
and engineers; plus manager, mechanics and electricians, and the protective
section. State Railway Battalion men not only pulled sentry duty at route
postings, but were seen at all tunnels and bridges the train would travel
through and on, at 20 mph to prevent both derailment and bothersome
rocking. Complained Alexander Mossolov dourly, "Railway journeys
involved a mass of complications!" Security was always uppermost. On
every trip the Imperial train took, both its older and newer versions were
sent out, to confuse would-be killers. The security cost was a stunning $1
million in modern terms, or 100,000 rubles in those days. The Tsar wanted
to expand the Imperial train's reach clear to faraway Siberia, in the distant
east. For this, Nicholas II deserves a great deal of the credit, as a farsighted
military leader in his own right. Nicholas II's achieved transcontinental
railroad went over 5,793 miles of both frozen tundra and grassy steppe.

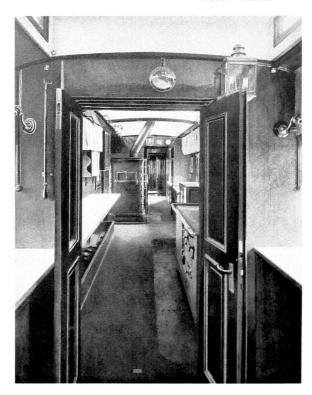

The kitchen carriage on the imperial train.

The Trans-Siberian Railway

Rivers were the main form of transport in Siberia of people and freight for approximately five months a year, until winter set in. Passengers and cargo were moved by horse-drawn sleighs over winter roads that were, in actuality, the same rivers, but then covered with frozen ice. Even the building of the Ob-Yenisi Canal still concluded with the same problem; only the iron horse of a tracked railroad would solve Siberia's chronic traffic dilemma. In 1851—following the completion of the St Petersburg–Moscow Railway—such ventures began to emerge concerning Siberia. Building the line was estimated to cost £35 million pounds Sterling, using 62,000 men that would include both Russian soldiers and Sakhalin convicted prisoners, and well as other slave laborers.

The construction was in seven separate sections, with work proceeding simultaneously on all. Russian engineers worked on both ends at once, each heading toward the center junction. In the Far East, it was laid northward along the right bank of the Ussuri River to Khabarovsk at the Amur River, named the Ussuri Railway. Running eastward, the Khabarovsk segment concluded in 1897.

Trains Ferried Over Water via Vessels

Trans-Siberian Railway construction commenced in March 1891, and in 1898, the first train arrived at Irkutsk and Lake Baikal's shores, 37 miles east of the city. Over single track ran engines with stacked chuffers to this break in the line at the lake. Two ice-breaking ferry vessels were built in the United Kingdom, and then shipped to Russia in pieces as so-called knock downs, where they were reassembled. SS *Baikal* was constructed in 1897, with the smaller ferry SS *Angara* in 1900, each making the four-hour-long water crossing to link the two opposing land-based railheads. Here again, sleighs also prevailed over ice connecting the two railheads. True railway men were utterly opposed to these waterborne cost-saving—but stopgap—solutions, arguing for permanent bridges to be constructed, for an uninterrupted railway. This was concluded under the premiership of Count Sergei Witte in 1903 to Vladivostock. It then veered south to Port Arthur via a train link with China. The 1904 completion of the Circum-Baikal Railway bypassed the ferries, but occasionally suffered both rock falls and even derailments, so the two ferry vessels were of necessity retained in service into 1916. Burned during the Russian Civil War, *Baikal* was survived by *Angara*. In 1905, a rail loop circling Lake Baikal was finished, and by 1915—with the Great War well underway—the Amur River line north of the Chinese frontier was also completed. Thus, an all-Russian throughway across the empire existed at last, the final great achievement of the reign of Tsar Nicholas II. Despite its low speeds and low train weights, the Trans-Siberian Railway did fulfill the longed-for promise of a railway to East Asia.

Railway Migration to Siberia, 1906–14

Nicholas' assassinated grandfather—Tsar Alexander II—freed the serfs in 1861. The building of the Trans-Siberian Railway resulted in an eastward migration of millions of freed peasants from both Western Russia and Ukraine, especially during 1906–14. An estimated four million arrived as colonizers of Russia's "Wild East."

Linkup with Chinese Lines

The lines forged ahead eastward, via the connecting Chinese Eastern Railroad/CER through Manchuria. The Amur River Line north of the Sino-Russian frontier was finished in 1916 and there existed at last the long desired continuous railroad St Petersburg–Vladivostock. Internally, the grid was but half done by the advent of the First Russian Revolution of February–March 1917, with the main line tracks all being laid in European—but not yet fully in Asian—Russia. Although the Asian part of the empire comprised 60 percent of its overall landmass—it had but 20 percent of its rail lineage.

Tsar Nicky's Pet Project

In March 1891—while traveling in the Far East as Tsarevitch—Nicholas at Vladivostock opened and blessed the commencement of the East Asian portion of it. He arrived from Japan on the closing leg of a global round trip. Later, *The Tsar's Train* was built at St Petersburg so that he could traverse his mammoth holdings in splendor and comfort. During 1891–1916, the Trans-Siberian Railway route started from the capital's Moskovsky Voksal, then ran via Moscow, Chelyabinsk, Omsk, Novosibirsk, Irkutsk, Ulan-Ude, Chita, and Khabarovsk to Vladivostok via southern Siberia. As a portion of the overall Trans-Siberian Railway, China and Russia collaborated on building the CER for a shorter passage to Vladivostok, run from its Harbin headquarters by an all-Russian administration. With 5,753 miles, the Trans-Siberian Railway and its parent railroad—the Transcontinental Russian Railway—linked hundreds of cities and towns across an unequaled seven time zones, in an unsurpassed eight days.

The Russo-Japanese War, 1904–05

Russia declared war on belligerent Japan, waged during 10 February 1904–5 September 1905, known as first the Manchurian Campaign, and later as the Russo-Japanese War. The Tsar's anti-Japanese war machine went east on the Trans-Siberian Railway, with a second line also to the Indian Ocean. The Chita-Vladivostok part of the Trans-Siberian Railway rolled through the then Chinese portion. With the war's stunning loss by Russia, it was determined that a 13 trains daily capacity had not been enough, as it was simply overwhelmed by too much traffic. It was also decided that, in future, the "Chinese" part must become Russian. The solution was the building of more basic bridging plus elevated crossings, and also the completion of the Circum-Baikal Railway. Upgraded as well was the entire lines' groundwork, with the Chinese portion parallel to another all-Russian route. The daunting Amur River was bridged during 1913–16. Of the one million Russian Army soldiers sent east to fight the

Japanese during 1904–05, 11,000 were Russian Railway Troops, for a manpower ramp-up from 125,000 to 1,300,000 by war's end.

The Japanese also built a military railway that they deployed far better than had the Russians theirs. Beginning with 300,000 troops, they ended the war victorious with 900,000. The Battle of Mukden encompassed 620,000 fighting men of both sides, employing a decade prior to the Great War of 1914 machine guns, barbed wire, torpedoes, telephone and telegraph communications, and at every level martial railroads. The Russo-Japanese War demonstrated that trains had forever altered the sheer scale of modern wars at the beginning of the Twentieth Century. The Trans-Siberian Railway enabled the war to occur as well as being a direct contributing cause. Simultaneous twin wars took place: the first on the actual battlefields, and the next on the lines to outdo the other side. This railway battle was won by the Japanese, and stunned the entire world as the first in which an Oriental people had beaten a white "western" nation.

Russia in the Great War: the All-Important Russian Gauge, 1914–18

The mainline railway route gauge of 4′ 8½″ was that standardized by 1915 of France, Germany, Holland, Belgium, Denmark, Austria-Hungary, Italy, Switzerland, Rumania, Turkey, Great Britain, Canada, and the United States. This permitted trains to travel from one country to another with the same rolling stock. However, the Russian railway gauge was 5′, necessitating a trans-shipment from one train to another at the frontier. Similar conditions are found in Spain and Portugal, where the standard gauge is 5′ 6″. Russia adopted her broader gauge so that—in case of invasion—the invader would not be able to run his rolling stock over her lines, as Germany, for instance would be able to do in the case of the railways of Belgium and France. This major gauge discrepancy aided Russia defensively, but hindered her with the Russian Army's twin invasions of enemy East Prussia in 1914. Norton in 1915 wrote:

> It should also be remembered that the reduction of a broad gauge to a narrow one is a much simpler matter from an engineering point of view than the widening of a narrower gauge into a broad one. In the former case, the existing sleepers, bridges, tunnels, platforms, etc., would still serve their purpose. In the latter case, fresh sleepers might have to be laid, bridges and tunnels widened or enlarged, and platforms and stations altered, the use of the broader gauge rolling stock thus involving an almost complete reconstruction of the railway lines.

In 1899, Prussia had established its communications troops that brought under a single command all railway technical units, plus the telegraph, and later as well the new Imperial Air Service, its commanding officer being an Army divisional general. On 25 March 1899, the single track Berlin-Jüterbog Railway—of but 44 miles—was built by the railway troops. It was felt that—in any war with Russia— technical units would duly convert the Russian 5′ gauge downward to the German 4′ 8½″ standard, or build instead special military lines to supplant those of Russia.

Lenin's Infamous "Sealed Train:" How the German Foreign Office Knocked Russia Out of the Great War, Starting in April 1917

James W. Gerard, the United States U.S. Ambassador to Berlin, recorded in his 1917 memoir:

> On 27 July 1915, I reported [to the State Department at Washington, DC] that I had learned that the Germans were picking out the revolutionists and liberals from the many Russian POWs, furnishing them with money, false passports, and papers, and sending them back to Russia to stir up a revolution.

He was right, and less than two years later, it went much further. On 5 April 1917, the German Foreign Office secretly set up a fund of 5 million Reich Marks to smuggle Russian Communist leader Vladimir Ulyanov [Lenin] into Russia from Switzerland, so that he could foment a Red revolution that would overthrow that country's pro-war Provisional Government, and withdraw Russia from the Great War. In March 1917, German Foreign Office State Secretary Arthur Zimmermann supervised the arrangements that led to the transfer of Lenin, his wife, and top members of his inner circle via rail from Zurich to St Petersburg. By this move, the Kaiser and his men helped unleash on Europe and the world the very Red revolution that all European monarchs had dreaded since 1848, again in the Paris Commune of 1871, yet again in the Russian revolt of 1905, and, finally in the collapses of 1917–18. Rarely has a single railway journey resulted in such an upheaval, and thus is worth inclusion here. Winston Churchill in his postwar book *The World Crisis* wrote:

> They [the Germans] transported Lenin in a sealed train like a plague bacillus … to Russia.

Under the terms of the secret German–Bolshevik pact the communists agreed to withdraw Russia from the war, and also to field a Russian Army to invade British India. Some in Lenin's entourage saw the train ride as a hidden trap, and feared that once inside Russia, they would be shot as German spies. The trip included 600 miles through Imperial Germany itself. As Lenin's party entrained at Zurich on 9 April 1917, they were met at the station by angry catcalls from other Russian exiles in the know: "Provocateurs! Spies! Pigs! Traitors! The Kaiser is paying for the journey! They are going to hang you!" The now-famous train had one green coach with eight compartments—three second class and five third class wagons—plus a baggage car, all overseen by a German Capt. von Planetz, who welcomed aboard Lenin and his Red comrades. It was Lenin's idea to "seal off" his party from its German escorts—and not the other way round—perhaps to distance them from the charge of being enemy agents, as transpired. The Germans stayed aloof in the third class compartment, drawing in white chalk a line on the floor! The only non-Russian allowed to cross it was the Swiss liaison Fritz Platten. With toilets at both end of the carriage, the Russians used one and their escorts the other. After all passengers were aboard, three of the compartment's four external doors were locked, with the fourth left free opposite that of the escort officers, on the German side of the chalked-in line. Some younger Reds sang the French Revolutionary song, the *Marseillaise,* its refrains echoing over the tracks of forested German Baden on the Baden State Railway into north Germany. All through Karslruhe, Offenburg, Stuttgart, and Mannheim, it rumbled on past deserted stations, with an engine switch occurring on the Prussia-Hesse line Mannheim-Frankfurt, the Reds' infamous "sealed train" having been awarded priority over all other internal German rail traffic.

At Halle, they transferred from the Saxon railroad to the Prussian line, and even the special train of Imperial Crown Prince Wilhelm was held up so that the little band of communists could pass on through to the Potsdam Station. The locked in Russians had their meals passed in to them, and there was a 20-hour layover in Berlin, the Kaiser's own capital. By now, 40 million gold Reichmarks had been invested in Lenin's journey, and there may even have been a secret intelligence meeting on the halted train with Lenin himself. The train was moved closer from Potsdam to Berlin's Stettin Station, in greater proximity to the site of the German Foreign Office on the Wilhelmstrasse in the downtown government quarter. This re-routing allowed Lenin to see the government quarter of his hated enemies. At Sassnitz on 12 April 1917, the Communists detrained to take the ferryboat *Queen Victoria* to board a night a train at Malmö for Stockholm in neutral Sweden. Next came a day trip though Finland to Beloostrov in Russia, where Lenin was hoisted onto the shoulders of workers on the first platform he reached. Re-boarding the train, his nervous followers still asked, however, "Are we going to be arrested in Petersburg?"

At a Cabinet meeting in the former Tsarist Imperial City, Provisional Government leader Alexander Kerensky—the man who had overthrown the Romanov dynasty—stated nervously, "Just you wait! Lenin is coming! Then the real thing will begin!" He was to be proven right. On Easter Monday, 1917, Lenin's infamous "sealed train" chugged into the later celebrated Finland Station. N. N. Sukhanov witnessed this tumultuous arrival and wrote the following account:

> The throng in front of the Finland Station blocked the whole square … scarcely letting the trams through … troops with bands were drawn up under Red flags near the side entrance, in the former Imperial waiting rooms.… Startling the mob and cutting through it, (there was) a strange, monster—a mounted searchlight …

In the station itself, there had been erected arches of triumph in red and gold every few yards for the platform above the mass of waiting people. There were also several guards of honor—soldiers, sailors, and newly formed Bolshevik-armed, civilian Red Guards, too. The wall graffiti announced, "Lenin arrives today. Greet him!" Already also underway, however, was the anti-Lenin-as-German-stooge campaign branding him a traitor. Lenin's train was late arriving in the former Tsar's own, personal station that stood ready now to welcome him in the name of the Petersburg Soviet at 11 p.m., as Lenin and his entourage stared out the car windows in stunned amazement at what they all thought was an incredible scene.

When the train halted, Lenin boldly stepped down first on to the platform, even as his reception committee rushed toward the car. Now the gala reception was in full swing, with bands both inside and out of the Finland Station booming the anti-monarchist Red anthem, that same *Marseillaise,* as earlier. Alexandra Kollantai personally handed Lenin a large bouquet of flowers, while officers bawled out orders to guards of honor that snapped into Present Arms! All very much in the style of the previous Imperialist platform welcomes.

> There thundered forth such a powerful, stirring, and hearty 'Hurrah!' as I've ever heard in my life [noted one eyewitness]. We approached the sailors. Observing the full ceremonial parade procedure, the ensign in command reported to Vladimir Ilyich, who looked at him perplexed. I whispered to him that the sailors wanted to hear him speak. Vladimir Ilyich walked past the guard of honor … took several steps back along the front rank of this guard of honor … halted, took off his (workers')

Vladimir Ilyich Ulyanov, better known by the alias Lenin (1870–1924), addressing a crowd in St. Petersburg.

hat," and spoke: "'Sailors! Comrades! We have to fight for Socialist revolution, to fight until the proletariat wins full victory! Long live the worldwide Socialist revolution!'"

Later, one angry Russian soldier—having heard him speak—said that:

We ought to stick our bayonets into a fellow like that! He must be a German, or he ought to be.

The Russian Civil War and Armored Trains, 1917–22

In the Russian Civil War of 1917–22, Red armored trains established Bolshevik control outward from then Petrograd to the 900 other Red Soviets across the country. They were used more in the Russian Civil War than in any other conflict—as well as cavalry. The 23 armored trains of 1918 rose to 100 by 1920. Bolshevik field commander Leon Trotsky ran the civil war from his mobile nerve center in just such an armored train. The conveyance had been termed by some military railway experts as the Russian Civil War's truly decisive tool in winning it for the Reds—thereby beating the monarchist counter-revolutionary Whites. They also negated the efforts of all the Allied Interventionist Powers—including the Japanese in Siberia.

Lenin launched the October Revolution of 1917 that overthrew Kerensky's Provisional Government, opposed then by the anti-Red, pro-Tsarist White Russian Army of Adm. Alexander Kolchak, headquartered at Omsk, where they fought the newly created Red Army on the Omsk Front. Behind the White lines, Red partisans blew up rail trackage as the civil war gradually ended.

The Railway Saga of the Czechoslovakian Legion, 1918–20

To secure the establishment of a postwar independent Czechoslovakian state, Czech and Slovak volunteer units were established in Russia during the Great War to fight the Germans alongside the Russian Army. Expanded, the unit became the 1st Division of the Czechoslovak Corps, or Legion. That October, it was again expanded by a second division of four more regiments to number almost 40,000 officers and men by 1918. The Czechoslovak Legion was deployed—with armored trains—along the Trans-Siberian Railway from Penza-Vladivostock, where it was to repatriated home by sea from the newly born Red state, but was delayed both by poor conditions on the line as well as by the Reds' demand that it surrender its arms, which was rejected. Following one such dispute on 4 May 1918 at Chelyabinsk Station, Trotsky ordered not only its

Zaamurets—armored trains—arose out of the Russian revolution. In 1918, the Bolsheviks had 23 such armored trains. By 1920, one in every 10 of the Red Army's artillery guns rested on one of its 103 rail-borne battleships.

A Zaamuret in Manchuria.

A Czech armored train, probably in Vladivostok.

disarmament, but also its arrest, resulting in what became known as *The Revolt of the Legions* of 25 May 1918. They were later joined by pro-Tsarist White Cossacks, with open warfare along the disputed Trans-Siberian Railway Pensa–Krasnoyarsk line.

Meanwhile, at Vladivostok, the Czechoslovak Legion commanding Gen. Mikhail Diterikjs overthrew the local ruling Red Soviet organization, and retraced the Czechoslovak Legion's earlier Trans-Siberian Railway route westward to rescue his forces still in combat on that front. In these early battles with the newly established Red Army, the Czechoslovak Legion easily beat Trotsky's rather raw units. On 12 July 1918, the 45,000-strong Legion took Omsk. By September 1918, the Legion had ejected the Red Army from all along the contested Trans-Siberian Railway, thus in effect becoming a foreign army running its own Russian railway line.

The Allied Intervention Corps, 1918–20

When the Allied Intervention Corps arrived at Vladivostock in fall 1918, it was welcomed ashore by a Czechoslovak Legion that still occupied this Russian Far Eastern port. By autumn 1918, the Corps numbered 70,000 Imperial Japanese Army troops; 829 British; 1,400 Italians; 5,002 Americans, and 107 French Colonial Vietnamese soldiers. Together with the Czechoslovak Legion, the Russian Whites, and Cossack warlord chieftains, the Corps waged a counter-revolutionary war against the Reds in order to strangle the new Red revolution, but they all failed.

Czech soldiers with their military band in Vladivostok, 1918.

The string of impressive initial military victories over the Reds, though—as well as the capture at Kazan on 5 August 1918 of the former Tsarist state gold reserves—led the Allies to fully support the new independent state that had been proclaimed at Prague on 28 October 1918. During the winter of 1918–19, the 61,000-man Czechoslovak Legion secured the Trans-Siberian Railway on the route Novonikolaevsk–Irjutsk. In this, they were aided as well by newly formed legions of Polish, Rumanian, and Yugoslav POWs freed from camps by the Legion, all now fighting against the Reds, but the tide turned against them. On 14 November 1919, the Red Army retook Omsk, with the beaten Whites retreating along the Trans-Siberian Railway, and aboard the Czechoslovak Legion trains was the Kazan gold bullion, later stranded on the line near Nizhneudinsk. On 7 February 1920, the Reds and the Czechoslovak Legion signed an agreement whereby the Legion was granted uncontested passage via the Trans-Siberian Railway back to Vladivostock, in return for surrendering the gold to the Soviets, "dozens" of Legion trains then being on the line. On 1 March 1920, the last Legion transport train exited Irkutsk, now hampered by the Japanese Army Expeditionary Force, as well as by Lieutenant General and *Ataman* of the Baikal Cossacks, Grigory Semenov's riders; the latter trying to detain the Legion until the arrival of the eastern Siberian Red Army to capture it intact. This failed, and the final units of the Legion departed from Vladivostok in September 1920 after six years of war in Russia. Statistically, 67,739 left Russia, including 3,004 officers; 56,455 enlisted soldiers; 6,714 civilians; 1,716 wives; 717 children; 1,935 foreigners, and 198 "others." In the Czechoslovakian Republic, the Legion veterans became the core of the new state army, while of others who came home, some joined the Czech Communist Party. For both the Great War and the Russian Civil War combined, the Czechoslovak Legion reported 4,112 men killed in action. Truly, theirs had been an epic journey home!

The Fall of the Romanov Dynasty via Railways, 1917–18

On 18 December 1916, the Tsar left Russian Imperial General Headquarters at Mogilev. This occurred when he heard that Father Grigori Rasputin had been murdered at St Petersburg—by monarchists trying to save the imperiled dynasty. The Tsar returned to Mogilev on 22 February 1917. Next, Nicholas received an ominous telegram from his consort Tsarina Alexandra—whom he had left behind to run the civil government while he waged war at the front. The text read: "Concessions inevitable. Many units gone over to the enemy. Alix." The Tsar sent 700 troops to the capital to restore order, to no avail. What this meant was that the hated democratic legislative body the *Duma* would have to be given shared powers to run both the government and the war, and that formerly loyal troops had joined the food rioters and workers who were in open civil revolt at the capital. Stunned, Nicholas decided to again return immediately to their home, the Alexander Palace, 15 miles outside the capital, at *Tsarskoe Selo*, leaving once more aboard the Imperial train. Originally, his planned route included Mogilev–Orsha–Vyazma–Likhoslavl, with an expected time of arrival at his home being 1 March 1917, at 3:30 p.m. Thus, from the later alleged "safety" of "Being in the middle of the Russian Army," the Tsar drove instead on his now revolution-held capital, hoping to restore order and also save his family. He took not a direct—but rather a roundabout— route home so as not to force troop and supply trains bound for the war from the line in his path. Even as he was traveling, the unbelievable happened: the Alexander Palace fell to the rebels! Worse followed suit for the Tsar personally in transit, when his own train was halted on the track at the Malaya Vishera Station by rebel soldiers armed with machine guns and artillery, about 100 miles south of Petrograd. In a hurried conference aboard his train, the Russian emperor decided instead to detour to Pskov, where he arrived at 8 a.m. at that town's station the same day, 1 March 1917. There, more bad news awaited him: whole units of the Russian Army had defected, including his very own, elite Imperial Guard. Faced with no military support at his capital, Nicholas decided that an entire *Duma*-appointed civil government would have to take his place ruling Russia. It would have its own premier for the first time, and thus not his, but even this drastic measure was now not enough. He received a wire from the capital that showed how far things had gone. In his diary, he wrote:

> A terrible revolution has broken out … I have been forced to arrest all the ministers … Do not send any more troops! … The measures you propose are too late. The time for them is gone. There is no return.

Next, the *Duma* decided that the Tsar must abdicate the throne, succeeded by his son and Heir Tsarevitch Alexei under a Regency of the Tsar's younger brother Grand Duke Michael, until Alexei turned 18 in 1923. Worse even still, the ultimate military authority at *Stavka*—the High Command of the Russian Army—concurred with this civilian political decision as well. Indeed, even all the lesser front combat commanders had already been polled, and they also agreed. Personally overwhelmed—and seemingly with nowhere to turn for support—Nicholas duly accepted the united advice of all his generals. Turning about from his coach window, Nicholas II announced his stunning decision:

I have decided that I shall give up the throne in favor of my son, Alexei. I thank you gentlemen for your distinguished and faithful service. I hope it will continue under my son.

A formal draft of an abdication was sent from *Stavka* at Mogilev to the Imperial train at Pskov, and His Majesty signed it. Now Emperor Alexei II, 12, was the legal Autocrat of all the Russias. The former Tsar then had second thoughts, conferred next with family physician Dr Fedorov, and changed his mind: due to his underage son's serious hemophilia internal bleeding medical condition of which most of the nation was unaware, Papa Nicholas decided that only by keeping his son with him could he receive the best care possible. Meeting with the two *Duma* delegates from Petrograd, Nicholas II announced that he was abdicating for his son as well, and in that case, Grand Duke Michael instead would succeed to the throne, just as Nicholas I had done with the death of his older brother Tsar Alexander I in 1825. He so amended the formal Abdication to reflect this new political change, it being signed on 2 March 1917 aboard the train.

After this dramatic 30 hours at Pskov, the Imperial train left to return to *Stavka*, arriving on 3 March 1917, so that the ex-Tsar—now known as Col. Nicholas Romanov— could bid a formal farewell to the generals and army there that had just left him in the lurch so suddenly. He waited for five days to do so, however, perhaps hoping that he could be, somehow, restored to power by this very same army. It was not to be, however. Disgusted, the now former Tsar noted in his diary, "All around me I see treason, cowardice, and deceit." Meanwhile—back at rebel-held Petrograd—his former soldiers all wore revolutionary Red armbands on their winter overcoats, and they were oddly torn between democracy and monarchy even so: "Oh, yes, we must have a republic, but we must have a good Tsar at the head!" To one weeping pro-Nicholas woman, a rebel explained, "They are not going to kill him! He has run away, that is all." The former Tsar's alleged "Allies" exulted in his fall. The United States became the first nation to recognize the new Russian provisional government, on 22 March 1917, less than two weeks before it, too, entered the war against the Central Powers. The loudest critics against the actions of the former emperor were the members of his extended family, and diplomats, one of whom lamented:

He had an army of 15 million men at his disposal! Fancy destroying a 300-year-old dynasty, and the stupendous work of Peter the Great, Catherine II, and Alexander I—what a tragedy, what a disaster!

Prior to Alexei's birth in 1904—the younger brother, Grand Duke Michael, had already been the Heir for the full decade of 1894–1904, but that was not going to happen now. Back at Petrograd, the two delegates bringing with them the former Tsar's abdication, were asked to address local railway workers, who were outraged when the pair called out, "Long live the Emperor Michael!" The train workers yelled back, "No more Romanovs—we want a republic!" The two offenders considered themselves lucky to leave the angry gathering at the railroad station with their lives. The new head of the provisional government—Alexander Kerensky—told "His Majesty Tsar Michael" that he had no troops to protect his life, and five minutes later, he also abdicated—on 3 March 1917—but hinted he might return if loyal troops could be found. That also was not to be, and thus his abdication as well was signed, with the Russian state having had a trio of legal monarchs during 2–3 March 1917.

With the dynasty thus ousted, Kerensky's government showed no fear that the old Tsar might yet change his mind again, and rally the troops at Mogilev to march by rail on Petrograd and take back his now lost throne. On 1 September 1917, Kerensky proclaimed Russia's first ever republic. At *Stavka*, the ex-Tsar's farewell Order of the Day was banned from publication by the *Duma*. Still, Nicholas did personally address his former generals on 8 March 1917 in the Mogilev hall. Fearing that the revolution would destroy the army, he cautioned them, "Remember, nothing matters but beating Germany!" From his own train window, the former all-powerful ruler could personally see Red flags at *Stavka*. On his second day back, his mother the former Tsarina—and since her late husband's 1894 funeral rail journey, Dowager Empress—Marie's train arrived and parked on a siding near Nicky's. Never having warmed to her son's German Hessian princess wife, the mother-in-law now blamed Alix for all that had befallen hapless Russia during her son's now ended reign of 24 years. For three days, mother and son met privately aboard her train, and went for short car trips in the area. Then came news that the new government had placed under house arrest at *Tsarskoe Selo* the now former Tsarina Alexandra. In addition, an express train was being sent from Petrograd bearing government commissioners to "escort" the also arrested Nicholas back to the capital via rail. After a final farewell lunch aboard her train, Nicholas left Marie and crossed the tracks back to his own drawing room car. The two trains headed off in opposite directions, mother and son never to meet again. As the former Tsar's train passed out of the Mogilev station, a general saluted Nicholas' carriage—and then bowed to that of the *Duma,* in this way acknowledging the passing of state power from one to the other.

At Tsarskoe Selo railway station, the railroad workers refused to provide any train for Alexandra to leave for safety elsewhere. Indeed, all the lines would be cut if she attempted to flee by rail, and in turn, all Petrograd

Russian Imperial family, 1914. *Left to right:* Grand Duchess Olga Nikolaevna, Grand Duchess Maria, Tsar Nicholas II, Tsarina Alexandra, Grand Duchess Anastasia, Tsarevitch Alexei, Grand Duchess Tatiana.

4th Rifles Guard Regiment, St. Petersburg, the guard of the Imperial family.

Grand Duchess Tatiana working outside Alexander Palace during internment at Tsarskoe Selo, 1917.

The Tsar and his family working in garden during internment at Tsarskoe Selo, 1917. The features of the Tsar are clearly visible.

lines were in the hands of the revolutionists: "We could not leave, and it was highly improbable that the Tsar could reach us," wrote Swiss family retainer Pierre Gilliard. Tsarskoe Selo was "protected" by a company of the Tsar's former Railway Regiment, and in all, there were deployed surrounding the Imperial estate 1,500 troops with an artillery battery. Bravely—and in the cold—Alix both addressed the men and personally trooped the lines, and the immediate danger passed that the men might not defend the palace if it was attacked by more hostile troops than they. Worried that her husband had not yet arrived, she told her friend, "Lili, the train is never late!" but it was. She awoke to find that all her "loyal" troops had simply vanished overnight. During her husband's personal telephone call, she confirmed this, being listened in on by the rebels, amid frightening rumors as well that both were to be tried by the new government. At her arrest, it was intimated that a British Royal Navy cruiser awaited the Imperial family at Murmansk to sail it to an exile in England. Instead— fearing riots in England should he grant his Russian cousins asylum—King George V abruptly rescinded his former—and already accepted—offer. It fell to Gilliard to tell the incredulous Alexei that he, too, had abdicated the throne of his ancestors, without his knowledge.

Upon the deposed ruler's arrival back home to "his" former station platform at Tsarskoe Selo, Nicholas was deserted by all his former officers and courtiers, being driven by car to meet once more his distressed wife. In time, Kerensky sent the entire Imperial family by rail east to Siberia away from the dangers surrounding it at the now seething capital, where he had his own difficulties with the local railway men. In place of the former ornate Imperial train, the former Royals traveled under a Japanese flag strangely in a *wagon-lits* coach of the International Sleeping Car Company, plus a restaurant car complete with the family's own wines, and, wrote Massie:

> a baggage compartment filled with favorite rugs, pictures, and knickknacks from the palace … In addition to the ladies and gentlemen of their suite, the Imperial family was accompanied to Siberia by two valets, six chambermaids, 10 footmen, three cooks, four assistant cooks, a butler, a wine steward, a nurse, a clerk, a barber, and two pet spaniels.

And that was not all. In addition to $500,000 worth of precious stones and jewelry brought along by the empress and her four daughters, the Tsar had with him all of the Kaiser's prewar personal letters to him, captured later and published by the Soviets as the infamous *Willy-Nicky Letters*. Thus far, the Tsar's own letters in return have not yet been published. A security colonel rode aboard the Imperial family's train as before, and this was followed by a second, bearing 330 guards. The trains rattled eastward through European Russia in the heat and dust. One afternoon Her Majesty received a delightful surprise as she sat near an open window, fanning herself from the hot sun overhead: a soldier handed her a cornflower through the open window. There was, after all, some common humanity through all their travail. All the stations along their route were manned by Red troops, all the blinds were pulled down, and no family member was allowed to appear at the windows. At Perm—just before the Urals— railway workers stopped their train, demanding to know who was aboard, but Kerensky's signed pass allowed it to go through. The air turned cool as their car entered the Ural Mountains, and for the very first time, the Imperial family saw from the windows the vast steppes of this remote part of their former domains. This included the actual village where their murdered holy man—Father Grigori—Rasputin had lived, Pokrovskoe, he having predicted long ago that one day they all would, eerily. They reached Tyumen on the River Tura and boarded the steamer *Rus* [Russia] for a voyage northeast on the Tura and Tobol Rivers, with their destination of Tobolsk still 200 miles further on. The Trans-Siberian Railway bypassed the city as a backwater, this explaining why they arrived there via Tyumen instead. At the Tobolsk Governor's House, they were now 190 miles away from the nearest railway station at Tyumen.

Meanwhile—following his successful October Revolution—Lenin seized all the railroad stations, starting at Petrograd. Nicholas now believed that both Lenin and Trotsky were German agents, and with them firmly in charge, he regretted for the first time after all that he had abdicated. After the Treaty of Brest-Litovsk was signed between the Reds and the Hohenzollerns in March 1918, the shocked former Tsar exclaimed, "I should never have thought that the Emperor William and the German government could stoop to shake hands with these miserable traitors, but they will get no good from it! It will not save them from ruin!"

The Kaiser's Alleged Railway Rescue Plot to Free the Imperial Family, 1918

According to one his most recent biographers, after the war, Wilhelm II insisted that:

> I did all that was humanly possible for the unhappy Tsar and his family, and seconded heartily by my Chancellor … I ordered my chancellor to get in touch with the Kerensky government via neutral channels, informing him that—if a hair of the Russian Imperial family's head

should be injured—I would hold him personally responsible, if I should
have the possibility of doing so.

While this does sound like the authentic, bombastic Kaiser speaking could
or did he actually do anything to effect a safe passage for his cousin?
Reportedly, Kerensky said he would provide a train if he could, but then
he was himself overthrown by the Bolsheviks, and was thereafter in flight
as a refugee seeking safety for his own life. Meanwhile, Lenin moved the
new Red government from the old Imperial capital of Petrograd back
to the ancient Russian center of Moscow. There, reportedly, German
Ambassador Count Wilhelm Mirbach opened negotiations with the Reds
seeking a safe exit from Russia for Nicholas II and his entire immediate
family by rail.

The longest surviving member of the Kaiser's immediate family was his
only daughter, Princess of Prussia, Duchess of Brunswick, Viktoria Luise.
In her 1977 memoirs she touched on her father's stated desire to see the
last of the Romanovs freed, even though they all despised him:

> Kerensky had chosen the remote west Siberian town of Tobolsk—that
> had no railway connections—as the Tsar's place of internment … The
> journey to Tobolsk lasted 13 days … Finally, the family was transferred
> to Ekaterinburg in the Urals … Gilliard sought out the British and
> Swedish consuls and urgently requested their aid … 'Steps have already
> been taken.' On the Bolshevist side, it was decided to put on a show trial
> for the Tsar and Tsarina.

That never took place. There was much more to it than that. In the winter
of 1918, there might well have been a passenger train plot concocted to
free the Imperial family and then spirit them out of the country by sea.
Starting on 26 April 1918, they were removed 200 miles further eastward
from Tobolsk to Ekaterinburg, but—at first, because Alexei was ill—His
Majesty was to be sent on ahead alone, to Moscow instead, so the empress
went with him, leaving the rest of the family back at Tobolsk. Politically,
the Tsar feared that the Reds wanted him at Moscow to sign the Treaty
of Brest-Litovsk that had ended the war with the Germans, with massive
losses of prestige, population, and territory. The Tsarina thought so, too,
and she was determined that she must be with him so that he would not
bend to this pressure, as he had the year earlier when he abdicated. Now,
the Tsar and Tsarina were literally returning the way that they had first
come, but this time in carts overland, escorted by Red cavalry into the
railway station town of Tyumen, where yet another special train awaited
them.

The Soviet official in charge of this next railway journey was Vasily Vakovlev, who during the 1905 anti-Tsarist uprising had robbed gold from a Russian mail train, to help fund the revolution that was then bloodily suppressed by Cossacks loyal to the regime. Now, Yakovlev was ordered to bring them to Moscow aboard Car 42 of the Samara–Zlatoust Railway under a 100-man guard. However, he feared that if he did so via Ekaterinburg—headquarters of the rival Ural Soviet—his prisoners might be taken from their train from him by force. To avoid that, he made the unilateral decision to go east to Omsk, as opposed to west to Ekaterinburg. Once at Omsk, he could then join the Trans-Siberian Railway's southern track segment, and next double back via Chelyabinsk–Ufa–Samara, and on safely to Moscow, thus still carrying out his ultimate destination orders. He confided this detour to his Imperial passengers, and—with the entire train darkened—slipped away from Tyumen at 5 a.m. steaming east for Omsk. There was one additional fact that he did not tell them, however: after Omsk there followed literally thousands of miles of cleared track all the way to the Pacific Ocean coast. Was he—or had he become— part of a monarchist railway plot to free them? His later Soviet accusers thought so. As he left Tyumen the information that he was going in the opposite direction was telegraphed to Ekaterinburg with the Ural Soviet immediately branding Yakovlev both an outlaw and "A traitor to the Revolution!" with warning telegrams also sent to all Soviet authorities that could be reached to stop this now "runaway" train. The Omsk Soviet swiftly sent troops to stop him at Kulomzino Station, 60 miles short of Omsk, surrounding it. Confronted with the accusations against him, Yakovlev kept his nerve, left the Imperial couple behind, and in a single unhitched car and engine, departed from Lyubinskaya Station, to face the Omsk Soviet himself. Calling Sverdlov personally at Moscow from Omsk by telephone, Yakovlev explained his actions. Sverdlov changed course, dropped Moscow as the destination, and told Yakovlev to hand over his prisoners instead to the Ekaterinburg Soviet. Back at the stranded train, he so informed Nicholas, who lamented, "I would have gone anywhere but to the Urals ... People there are bitterly hostile to me." Yakovlev duly turned over Their Majesties—referred to as, "the cargo"—to the Reds at the Ekaterinburg II Shartash Station. Many of these particular trips suffer from being described in a number of differing accounts and even conflicting dates. Still, the Uralite Reds may very well thus have thwarted any of the Moscow Bolsheviks' plans to send the Royals abroad as part of a secret deal with Imperial Germany. Significantly, when they arrived at Ekaterinburg, no concrete plans had been made to house them there.

Yakovlev indeed did defect to the Whites six months later, leading his Red critics to again assert that his "change of direction" had all the while been part of the Moscow monarchist-concocted attempt to free the Tsar, take him to the Pacific, and release him to a British Royal Navy warship for transportation of the Royals to exile in the UK.

In his 1967 work, Massie disputed this, suggesting that Yakovlev as Moscow's agent simply found himself enmeshed between these rival western and eastern Soviet authorities. Only the Germans could have saved the Russian Imperial family at this point. Their army was even then occupying the former Imperial Russian domain of Ukraine. At that point, the Hindenburg–Ludendorff duo did not want either Petrograd or Moscow, but—had they so chosen instead—could have taken both cities and deposed Lenin's government. Thus, Tsarist plotters at Moscow had contacted Kaiser Wilhelm's just appointed new ambassador, Count Mirbach. Reportedly, he even told them, "Be calm. I know all about the situation in Tobolsk, and when the time comes, the German Reich will act." After all, he was speaking as the official representative of the very same German Foreign Office that had brought Lenin himself via rail from Sweden to Petrograd in April 1917. Now, however, the Germans feared that Lenin's revolution might spread to Germany's own Social Democrats, with urgings to "get rid of your Tsar!" as was already being said widespread among the armies on the Russian-German front lines to the west. Thus, the German Foreign Office was interested in overthrowing the Bolsheviks first, restoring some sort of Tsarist regime that would honor the Brest-Litovsk agreement, and maybe even become friendly with Germany again. Might this happen under a restored Romanov regime, with or without Nicholas II? It was Count Mirbach, therefore, who had urged that the Imperial family be brought to Moscow—within reach of the German Army, at least theoretically, anyway. Massie contended that Sverdlov secretly agreed to Mirbach's veiled threat demand, in order to prevent a full-scale German invasion that would result in the overthrow of the Red regime in its infancy, just as Churchill was also hoping would happen via the Allied Siberian Intervention. Yakovlev, therefore, was acting in this case as Sverdlov's direct agent—to a point. Behind the scenes, Sverdlov could order the Ekaterinburg Soviet to seize the Tsar "on its own" instead, thus giving Sverdlov a face-saving escape hatch with Count Mirbach and his boss, the Kaiser. In this way, Sverdlov made a double betrayal: of the Germans and of his own man, Yakovlev. As this double game was unfolding around him—with or without his connivance—it is also possible that Yakovlev decided mid-stream to change horses and take the Tsar to freedom on his own. Incredibly surviving yet another two full decades, Yakovlev was finally executed by the Reds in 1938.

Furious, Count Mirbach passed on from the Kaiser an offer to crown any Romanov family member in the Crimea as the next Tsar who would agree to sign the treaty already sanctioned by Trotsky, but none could be found to do so. When the German diplomat was approached yet again by Russian monarchists to rescue Nicholas and the rest of the family now also at Ekaterinburg, he declined:

> The fate of the Russian emperor is in the hands of his people! Had we been defeated, we would have been treated no better. It is the old, old story—woe to the vanquished!

Count Mirbach was assassinated in his Moscow Embassy on 6 July 1918, reportedly by Left Socialist-Revolutionary Byumkin, who believed that Lenin had betrayed them to the Germans. Allegedly, the hapless count was simply, "knocked on the head by a worker"—or might the assassin have been sent by the vengeful Lenin, Trotsky, or Sverdlov? Less than six months later—in November 1918, the Kaiser himself—the victor over Russia at Brest-Litovsk—was to be overthrown in a joint civilian-military coup of his combined political left and right in circumstances eerily similar to Nicholas' own forced abdication.

Having arrived at Ekaterinburg's main municipal railroad station— home of the worst anti-Tsarist Soviet in his former realm—"Bloody Nicholas" and the "German Woman" Alexandra in their coach heard the soldiers and mob yelling outside, "Show us the Romanovs!" so it was moved for their safety to another platform at an outer station. Alighting from the carriage having completed his last train ride, the Tsar carried his own bags to a waiting car to their final house of imprisonment, where—as a symbol of hope—his wife Alix drew a swastika on a dusty window and dated it: 30 April 1918. They had less than 90 days to live.

Massacre at Ekaterinburg, 16–17 July 1918

On 12 July 1918, the Ural Soviet allegedly decided to execute the entire Imperial family and its remaining court retainers within three days due to the nearness to Ekaterinburg of the rapidly advancing Czech Legion. Yakov Yurovsky commanded the brutal *Cheka* murder squad of 13 that killed them all at midnight on 16–17 July 1918 with pistols, rifle butts, and fixed bayonets in the basement of the Ipatiev House, after he read their death sentence aloud to them. Accounts differ as to how and in exactly what ways the Imperial Couple died first, and also on the order of who succeeded them in death, including a family cocker spaniel dog. Yurovsky claimed that he shot the Tsar himself. Reportedly—over the next three days—all the bodies were stripped naked, cut to pieces with axes and saws, and doused with

German Army officers in spiked helmets greet the Russian Communist Bolshevik negotiators for the Treaty of Brest-Litovsk in Poland in January 1918. Russia's chief negotiator—Leon Trotsky—is in the dark fur cap and overcoat at center. *Library of Congress*

both gasoline and sulfuric acid to destroy their physical facial features and identities, and every single detail of this grisly crime has been debated ever since. The final gory assize was to cover up what even the shamefaced Soviets themselves decades later admitted had been a foul and reprehensible deed by any and all moral standards. Yorovsky dated his official report at 17 July 1918, 1:15 a.m., asserting that 11 people had been killed in all.

U.S. Ambassador to Germany James W. Gerard, 1913–17

Noted American attorney James Watson Gerard (1867–1951) was a political appointee of the Wilson Administration, serving as U.S. Ambassador to Germany during 29 October 1913–5 February 1917. During 4 August 1914–5 February 1917, Ambassador Gerard found himself in the rather interesting position of observing Imperial Germany at war from *inside* the Second Reich.

Ambassador Gerard first met His Majesty when he presented his credentials to the Kaiser following the usual half-hour train ride from Berlin to the New Palace at Potsdam outside the Reich capital in 1913.

Prior to the outbreak of the Great War, Gerard remembered that:

It came to light that the Prussian State Railways were used as a means of discriminating against ... American oil [that] came to Germany through the port of Hamburg, and the Galician and Rumanian oil through the frontier town of Oderberg. Taking a delivery point equally distant between Oderberg and Hamburg, the rate charged on oil from Hamburg to this point was twice as great as that charged for a similar quantity of oil from Oderberg. I took up this fight on the line that the company must be compensated for all of its property ... [and] for the goodwill of its business that it had built up through a number of years by the expenditure of very large sums of money [with then Imperial Chancellor Theobald von Bethmann-Hollweg] ... I also said that I thought they [the Germans] had done enough for the Germans interested in the Galician and Rumanian oil fields when they had used the Prussian State Railways to give these oil producers an unfair advantage over those importing American oil. Shortly after this, the question of the creation of this oil monopoly was dropped, and naturally has not been revived during the war....

He claimed as well that the same tactic was used against American mineral oil, as well as, "Other articles such as wood, that otherwise might have be imported from America." Ambassador Gerard recalled as well in 1913 that:

Undoubtedly, the Germans based great hopes upon the Baghdad Railway that was to carry their influence to the east, and even threatened the rule of Great Britain in Egypt and India. Undoubtedly, there was talk, too, of a Slav railroad to run from the Danube to the Adriatic that would cut off Germany from access to the Southern Sea. Francis Deloisi the Frenchman in his book ... says, "In a word, the present Balkan War is the work of Russia, and the Danube Asiatic Railway is a Russian project. If it succeeds, a continuous barrier of Slav peoples will bar the way to the Mediterranean of the path of Austro-German expansion from the Black Sea to the Adriatic, but here again, the Romanovs confront the Habsburgs, the Austro-Serb conflict becomes the Austro-Russian conflict, two great groups are formed, and the Balkan conflict becomes the European conflict."

This was exactly what happened in July 1914 when the Reich sided fully with Austria versus Serbo-Russia, and the Great War resulted. Added Gerard:

Another reason for an immediate war was the loan by France to Russia made on condition that additional strategic railways were to be constructed by the Russians in Poland. Although this money had been received, the railways had not been constructed at the time of the opening of the Great War.

Speaking of this situation, the Russian Gen. Kuropatkin—in his report for the year 1900—said:

> We must cherish no illusions as to the possibility of an easy victory over the Austrian Army ... Austria had eight railways to transport troops to the Russian frontier while Russia had only four; and, while Germany had 17 such railways running to the German–Russian frontier, the Russians had only five.

After the Reich declared war on Russia on 1 August 1914, she did so as well on France on the 3rd. Britain retaliated by doing so against Germany on the 4th, with her own ally Imperial Japan following suit as well on the 23rd. Gerard left vivid impressions of the departures of the trio of now Allied ambassadors as they left Berlin via rail:

> On the day the Russian ambassador left, I sent my automobile to take him to the station. The chauffeur and footman reported to me that the police protection was inadequate, that the automobile was nearly overturned by the crowd, and that men jumped on the running board and struck the ambassador and the ladies with him in the face with sticks. His train was due to leave at 1:15 p.m. ... instead of going to Russia, was headed for Denmark.

When news circulated in Berlin that Great Britain had declared war on the Reich:

> The rage of the population ... was indescribable ... I went to the station to say goodbye to the French Ambassador Jules Cambon. The route from the French Embassy by the Brandenburg Gate to the Lehrter railway station was lined with troops and police, so that no accident whatever occurred. There was no one at the station except a very inferior official from the German Foreign Office ... Cambon instead of being sent out by way of Switzerland—whence of course the road to France was easy—was sent north to Denmark. He was very badly treated on the train, and payment for the special train—in gold—was exacted from him by the German government ... Sir Edward [Goschen, the British ambassador],

his staff, and the British correspondents left early next morning, about 6 a.m.

Now, others wanted to leave as well.

> I arranged—with the very efficient help of Lanier Winslow—for special trains to carry Americans to Holland. Trains were run from Switzerland, Munich, and Karlsbad across Germany to Holland, and from Berlin were run a number of trains to Holland … special trains by the Railroad Department of the German government.

On 2 August 1914, the U.S. Embassy duly announced the special trains for Americans to the Dutch border:

> Other trains will probably be arranged from time to time … All civil passengers are ejected from trains when troops require accommodation. It is better to wait for special trains arranged for by the Embassy …

This was instead of relying on normal German passenger rail service during the first few hectic days of wartime life in the Second Reich. The first train of Americans bound for home left for Holland from Berlin's Charlottenburg station on 13 August 1914. The next day, he commented that the Kaiser "abandoned Berlin" himself for the Western Front, to Pless in Silesia in 1916, and back to the West during 1917–18. Angry that U.S. shipping was supplying the Allies with war materials, His Majesty refused to see the American ambassador, even for a hurried railway platform hello and farewell in March 1915. That October, Gerard was granted an audience at the Potsdam New Palace on 22 October 1915.

Sweden remained neutral, and Gerard suggested this rather interesting reason why:

> I believe that this exchange of the heavily wounded between the Germans and the Russians was the factor that prevented the entrance of Sweden into the war. These wounded men traversed the whole length of Sweden in the railway, and the spectacle afforded to the Swedish population of these poor stumps of humanity—victims of war—has quite effectually kept the Swedish population from an attack of unnecessary war fever.

Gerard praised German women thus:

> They engaged in Red Cross work … and the first day of mobilization saw a number of young girls at every railway station in the country

with food and drink for the passing soldiers ... At railway junctions and terminals in the large cities, stations were established where these Red Cross workers gave a warm meal to the soldiers passing through. In these terminal stations, there were also women workers possessed of sufficient skill to change the dressings of the lightly wounded.

On his rail trip to the Western Front of 28 April 1915, Ambassador Gerard remembered that:

We were given a special salon car ... As we neared the front via the line running through Saarbrücken, our train was often halted because of long trains of hospital cars on their way from the front to the base hospitals in the rear; and as we entered France, there were many evidences of the obstinate fights that had raged in this part of the country in August 1914. Parts of the towns and villages that we passed were in ruins, and rough trench lines were to be discerned on some of the hillsides. At the stations, weeping French women dressed in black were not uncommon sights.... The fortress city of Metz through which we passed seemed to be as animated as a beehive. Trains were continually passing.... The Great General Headquarters of the Kaiser for the Western Front is in the town of Charleville-Mézières.... We were received at the railway station by several officers, and escorted in one of the Kaiser's automobiles.... The emperor had been occupying a large villa in the town of Charleville until a few days before our arrival. After the engineer of his private train had been killed in the railway station by a bomb dropped from a French airplane—and after another bomb had dropped within 100 yards of the villa occupied by the Kaiser—he moved to a red brick chateau situated on a hill outside of Charleville....

In 1916, the American ambassador was shocked to learn of the large Belgian populace deported for forced labor to the Second Reich.

The military did not propose to have a hostile population at their backs who might cut the rail lines of communication [as in France during 1870–71] telephones and telegraphs, and that for this reason, the deportation had been decided on.

This decision was taken by Ludendorff. The Quartermaster General was especially worried about this in case the BEF broke through German lines and overran Belgium. In January 1917, he and Chancellor Bethmann-Hollweg discussed possible American overtures to the Allies regarding peace. When the U.S. ambassador asked of him what he meant by "guarantees" he wanted from the Belgians, the chancellor rattled off a lengthy list of demands, among them:

> We must have possession of the railroad lines ... We must be allowed to retain a large army in Belgium.... and on and on.

On 4 February 1917, America broke diplomatic relations with Imperial Germany. Gerard described his departure with the Embassy staff from Berlin thus:

> We were about 120 persons in all on this train [this also included American residents] that left the Potsdamer station at 8 p.m.... [There was no demonstration whatsoever against them]. There was a large crowd in the station to see us off. All the Spanish Embassy, Dutch, Greeks, and many of our colleagues from Central and South America were there [as well as four German Foreign Office members]. As the train pulled out, a number of the Americans left in Berlin who were on the station platform raised quite a vigorous cheer. Two officers had been sent by the Imperial government to accompany us on the train. I had ordered plenty of champagne and cigars to be put on the train, and we were first invited to drink champagne with the officers in the dining car. Then they joined us in the private salon car that we occupied at the end of the train.... The journey was uneventful. Outside some of the stations, a number of people were drawn up who stared at the train in a bovine way, but who made no demonstration of any kind. We went through Württemburg, and entered Switzerland by way of Schaffhausen. The two officers left us at the last stop on the German side ... At the first station on the Swiss side, a body of Swiss troops were drawn up, presenting arms, and the colonel commanding the Swiss Army ... attended by several staff officers, came on the train and traveled with us to nearby Zurich.... At Zurich, we left the German special train, and were met on the platform by some grateful Japanese, the American consul, and a number of French and Swiss newspaper reporters, thus ending our exodus from Germany.

Back in the U.S., former Ambassador Gerard published his diplomatic tenure memoirs later in 1917:

> The third winter of the war—owing to a breakdown of means of transportation and want of laborers—coal became very scarce.... In Berlin, even the elephants from *Hagenbeck's Show* were pressed into service to draw the coal carts from the railway stations.... The new underground road [subway] in Berlin is being built largely by woman

The original Big Bertha was a howitzer mainly designed by Krupp's Director of design, Professor Fritz Rausenberger, and his predecessor, Director Max Dreger (1852–1929). This later rail-mounted 'La Grosse Bertha' was at Brussels, *c.* 1915 and taking a liberty with the name, which came into generic use for German large guns.

labor. This is not so difficult a matter in Berlin as in New York, because Berlin is built upon a bed of sand, and the difficulties of rock excavation do not exist. Women are employed on the railroads, working with pickaxes on the roadbed. Women drive the great yellow carts of Berlin. There were women guards on the underground road, women conductors on the tramways, and women even became motormen on the tramcars.

Ambassador Gerard's memoirs end on a humorous railroad note:

The "escaped" [British] prisoner took with him some sandwiches made of the bread he had received in Ruhleben, and most incautiously ate one of these sandwiches in a railway station. He was immediately surrounded by a crowd of Germans anxious to know where he had obtained the *white bread,* and in this way, was detected, and returned to prison.

U.S. Naval Railroad Guns versus the German Paris Gun, 1918

Railway guns by general definition consisted of both large guns and howitzers mounted on—and then fired from—specially built flatbed railroad car platforms. During the First World War all of the major power combatants deployed them, varying by degrees in caliber mm measurements. Although the Allies—or Entente Powers as the Germans called them—did not name their own railway guns, they had and deployed them nonetheless: 14 by the French Army, four by the BEF, more used by the AEF, and even one for the Italians. Of all the First World War armies, however, it was the Germans who, with their eight guns, established world records of size, range, ordnance, cost, and resources consumed that could have been better used for other, more conventional weaponry instead.

The German Army named them, as it did its various service regiments. These included: *Nathan, Samuel, Peter Adalbert, Theodor Otto, Theodor Karl, Bruno, Kurfürst* [Prince Elector], *Max*, and one of the largest of all—*Wilhelmsgeschutz*.

As part of a program of on-going enhancements Professor Fritz Rausenberger of the Krupp firm had, by 1915, fused modified naval gun designs to railway mounts that became the first in a later series of such long-range railway guns. A pair of them was used against the French forts at Verdun starting on 21 February 1916, firing from a distance of 20 miles away. Noted Dooly, "After a few shots, the rails of the marshaling yard were standing in the air like twisted fragments of wire."

As the Battle of Verdun intensified, both the French and the Germans used railway guns to bombard their enemies' rear areas, as well as to demolish both forts and deep tunnel and bunker sites. The French Army's 400 mm *Schneider* guns helped to retake their own former *Ft. Vaux*, while at the Third Battle of Ypres, a brace of BEF 14″ railroad cannons—*Boche-Buster* and *Scene-Shifter*—waged comparable long-distance bombardments against the Germans.

Eight such American naval railway guns encased in armored mounts constructed by the Baldwin Locomotive Works with a range of 24 miles were engaged by September 1918 in France. By the time of the November 1918 Armistice, these mighty artillery tube cars were seen by all the various field armies engaged as *the* supreme means of conveyance, with the U.S. Coast Guard Artillery alone using 71 guns within 10 American regiments, in size from 14″ down to 190 mm (7½″), all built in France.

Oddly, the popular name of *Big Bertha* given to *Wilhelmsgeschutz*—the German Paris gun—is a misnomer. The true *Big Bertha* was a very heavy 420 mm (16½″) howitzer that started with overwhelming success in 1914 against the Belgian forts on the river and near Antwerp. *Big Bertha*, also known as *Kurze Marine Kanone* was a direct derivative of the most far-reaching artillery of those days—the ship's cannon.

The Germans began work on their "super gun" in 1914, initially thinking that it would be stationed at a fixed location and to shoot at one target—Dover. From Cap Gris Nez in France, the narrowest part of the Channel to England is 33 kilometers (21 miles). To this end—wind and weather permitting—the gun required a firing range of at least 37 kilometers. German field artillery was defined with its radius of about 15 kilometers and therefore utterly unsuitable. The 380 mm ship cannon Max Langer, however, had a much greater theoretical firing range of 28 kilometers (theoretically, because the ships could shoot only under sub-optimal angles of 30 degrees). Based on Max Langer and a second, slightly larger experimental ship's cannon, the Krupp firm began experimenting with technical improvements that could boost the range a few kilometers.

It worked far better than the Krupp firm had dared to hope. Firing tests showed that a combination of a large firing angle (between 50 and 55 degrees) together with bright, sleek projectiles obtained much better results. It was decided on the basis of the tests and calculations to develop a gun with an ultra-long range of fire. Led by the brilliant Professor Fritz Rausenberger came the first real super cannon—*Wilhelmsgeschutz*. The gun was 34 meters long, weighed 200 tons and had a caliber of 210 millimeters. It could only be transported by rail. The wall thickness at the height of the breech (bottom impact) amounted to forty centimeters. The final construction was so heavy that Rausenberger had it strengthened against sagging by a steel truss structure.

In the interior of the firing tube the first 18 meters were in slightly spiraling grooves which corresponded with cams on the projectile. The grooves gave it the rotary motion required for stability during flight. To fire the approximately one-meter-long shells—equipped with an aerodynamic point—required a powder charge of between 150 and 200 kilograms; cartouches packed in with a total length of nearly three meters (10′). The *Wilhelmsgeschutz* was operating at the outer limits of technical feasibility. Each shot created so much wear within the rear part of the barrel that later designs had much thicker walls. The brute-force of the design in the later versions led to an amazing maximum firing range of more than 120 kilometers (75 miles). The Teutonic-sounding moniker of *Wilhelmsgeschutz* was the German name for the gun, given to honor Kaiser Wilhelm II.

On 21 March 1918, Paris suddenly experienced a "silent death" that seemed to erupt from nowhere out of the early morning calm, evidence of yet another German terror weapon of mysterious origin. Remembering the bombardment that destroyed Belgian Liège in 1914, Parisians dreaded that their beautiful City of Light might now suffer the same dire fate. They were not wrong, either, as the deadly explosions truly did emanate from over a long distance and from a top-secret firing site. French air reconnaissance reported that a huge, 210-pound shell was thus being lobbed across 75 miles by a sinister new piece of enemy artillery, discovered later to be a

This French 320 mm railway gun uses sliding recoil. The jacked-down sleepers are just about visible.

A British 9.2 inch railway gun at Maricourt, September 1916.

mammoth railroad gun in the dense Compiègne Forest: the so-called Paris Gun. In all, it allegedly claimed 876 casualties and 256 killed in action, mainly Parisian civilians.

To combat this fearsome new monster were the already promised U.S. Navy former battleship turret guns mounted on railroad carriages that boasted 14″ weapons to return fire. Of this, French Army Gen. Henri Aubert was certain, and he therefore pressed anew for their delivery from the commander of the new American Expeditionary Force, Gen. John J. "Black Jack" Pershing.

Built as spare naval rifles for the new 27,000 ton U.S. battlewagons *Oklahoma* and *Texas* class ships of 1912–24, the mighty guns were even then *en route* fro France by sea, reconfigured as long range naval artillery mounted on railroad car mobile platforms. It was believed that these 25″ behemoths were, indeed, the *only* counter weight to the lethal Paris Gun, and—by smashing targets behind German lines—both could and would end this second siege of Paris. Conceived in April 1917 and led by Rear Adm. Charles Pershall Plunkett, the U.S. batteries had not arrived yet in France by August 1918, by which time more than 1,000 Parisians had been either killed or wounded by German shells. The mounting of the giant 14″ naval guns on to their specially designed cars was speeded up. The operation had been contracted on 13 February 1918 to the U.S.-based American Steel Company, and was to include an entire support train with loading crane, ammunition, crew living quarters, supplies, mess, radio, and logistical coaches all. As soon as the guns arrived in France, Allied scouting planes deployed to locate the enemy's weapon, and would also serve as aerial forward observers for the U.S. naval railway guns. Gen. Pershing wrote after the war that:

> Meanwhile … our large caliber naval guns had advanced, and were skillfully brought into position to fire upon the important lines at Longuyon, Verdun, and Montmédy. The strategic goal that was our highest hope was gained. We had cut the enemy's main line of supply and communication, and nothing but surrender or armistice could save his army from complete disaster.

But that was not of much immediate assistance to the vexed Parisians at the moment! Due to the naval guns' super heavy weight, attached to the firing platform car's bottom were six-wheel bogies to support them. Had the war gone on beyond 1918, it was already planned that 30 such guns would be in France by March 1919, with 60 specially rated sailor gun crew members manning each nine-car support train. As with all Gen. Pershing's other BEF units, the rail-mounted naval guns as well would be under

The 'Paris Gun'—*Wilhelmsgeschutz*—firing at an angle of approximately 40 degrees.

American command, not French. Even so French railway officials delayed the authorization for the heavy rolling guns' transit over the country's railroad system, for fear of damaging the tracks. In due course they were, finally, on their way to the front. Not without validity, the French railroad men rightly worried, though: would the cars' massive weight simply be too much for their trackage and bridges? Asked one authority:

> Could their roadbeds sustain the weight of railroad cars three times heavier than French rolling stock?

Indeed, as they passed over, the French and Americans cringed in silence as bridges "creaked and groaned beneath them," the roadbeds crumbling as the American guns at but six mph traveled via rail 350 miles to their firing posts, with even the smallest upgrade slowing down the trains ever more. Special care was given by the engineers to every single curve on the line, the same being true as well of tunnels, crossovers, and viaducts. As the first train arrived at the Helles–Mouchy firing site, onlookers marveled at the awesome 60′ long and 14″ diameter gun barrels.

Nor were the Germans caught napping, as their own Imperial Air Service scout planes overhead were diligently shadowing this initial train, its Baldwin steam engine producing clouds of smoke, bringing the USN 1st and 2nd Batteries closer to their own Paris Gun. That weapon's gunners now dreaded the arrival of their opposite numbers. Berlin was worried as well, especially as the High Command was not entirely satisfied with what was also known as *The Krupp Works Gun,* designed and built by the world famous armorial gun maker of Essen, in Germany's industrial basin, the Ruhr. Noted an excellent technical *Report* by authority Owen Gault:

Due to the extreme 92′ length of its barrel, it was required to be externally braced to avoid barrel droop and insure any degree of accuracy at its maximum range of 80 miles. But even then, the extreme distance that the shell had to travel saw its accuracy affected by the earth's rotation—a phenomenon known as the Corolis effect—mandating that the spot at which it had been aimed would have *moved* substantially during the 170 seconds the shell took to reach its target. This phenomenon—combined with the unknown winds aloft as the shell reached its maximum height of 25 miles—made trajectory calculations something less than an exact science, with the result that the gun was only effective against city-sized targets. Due to its 256-ton weight, the gun carriage proved to be unwieldy to operate. In addition to a number of characteristics that slowed its reloading cycle, the barrel core itself had to be replaced after 60–65 firings, because the rifling wore out fast, due to the high, 5,200 fps velocity of the shell.

Thus, following each discharge, its bore must be minutely measured, so that the succeeding shell—built with successively numbered larger diameters to offset the barrel groove wear—would properly seat in the breech block. By the time 65 firings had been made, the shell's diameter had been increased from 8.3–9.2″! Built in two parts with the last 20′ of barrel having no grooved rifling, the extension itself was inserted into a 380 mm Long Max barrel to assist boosting the shell's flight. Manned by a gun crew of 80 German sailors, the gun's recoil alone reportedly sent it scooting more than 150 feet down the tracks. To help conceal the ear-splitting noise of each shot fired, the Paris Gun was surrounded by a cordon of large bore Skoda (Czech-made) howitzers that would fire in concert with the big gun, to help smother its unique sound.

Like its rival USN railroad guns, the Paris Gun, too, was mounted on a huge railway carriage, and then held the global record for any human built object shooting into the sky. It was then also the world's largest rifled gun. Again suddenly—and also once more without warning—dazed Parisians awoke on 28 September 1918 to an unreal silence. Up to then, 20 or more daily shells for almost a total of 400 in all had fallen and exploded. People wondered why or how their hated enemy's weapon was attacking them no more. The simple answer was that the initial pair of USN guns had arrived onsite five days earlier, on 23 September 1918. Added the Gault *Report:*

Despite all their training, it took the gun crew time to get their elevation pits dug, and structural steel shoring foundations built. Unable to traverse

The U.S. Navy 14″ 50 caliber railway guns were spare U.S. Navy Mk 4 14 inch mounted on railway cars and operated by U.S. Navy crews in France in the closing months of the First World War. *Library of Congress*

laterally ... [they were] ... only able to elevate 43 degrees without having a pit dug under them into which the gun could recoil. The railway guns had to be positioned on curved tracks to obtain the proper azimuth to the target. If no suitable trackage could be found, U.S. Army engineers assigned to the train had the necessary rail, ties, and ballast to build short rail spurs to provide the correct azimuth to the target.

On 5 September 1918—the first Marne battle's fourth anniversary—the USN guns at last opened fire against the Paris Gun. With the ground below heaving and shaking, a trio of the five U.S. Naval gun batteries opened up with 1,000-pound High Explosive, armor piercing rounds. Not only was the Paris Gun thus assaulted, but German occupied rail terminals at Laon, Conflans, and Montmédy, were, too. This had the practical effect of bringing to a dead stop all train traffic behind German lines. The USN sailor gunners exulted when told that their just fired rounds were hitting their targeted foe 20–23 miles behind the German Army's front lines at Soissons and the Marne River! This was long-range gunnery at its very best, and elation was felt among both American services in France, with many more targets soon identified that could not be assaulted via any other ordnance modality. Paris was never so struck again. Meanwhile, Allied air reconnaissance confirmed that the Paris Gun was secretly taken down and returned to the Second Reich, as the Compiègne Forest locale sheltering it began itself to be flattened by the sailors' deadly artillery fire.

"I will be damned if we did not scare the Huns away!" asserted one chief gunner's mate.

Thus ended the five-month-long Parisian wave of terror, with the Krupp firm taking their gun apart—and ordering it to be destroyed with all plans and related gear—to keep the closely-guarded secret weapon away from the Allies. At war's real end—the signing of the Versailles Treaty of 28 June 1919—the beaten Germans were officially denied any re-building of the deadly unit. Back at Compiègne Forest, the Allies saw only bits and pieces of debris that the crushing USN shelling had left in its wake. The USN guns continued to be successfully deployed on the Western Front, severely damaging German front trains and bases, as well as routes, bridges, and ammunition dumps. In all—over the course of 25 days in combat—U.S. naval rifles sent skyward 782 14″ shells hurtling forward 20–24 miles each. Indeed, it was a shell fired from Naval Battery 4 that was allegedly the last fired in the First World War, at a cost in American losses of one sailor killed, and six wounded by enemy shrapnel. Both the German Army Paris Gun and the USN railway guns made armament history, with the latter returning home to serve as U.S. Coastal Artillery, but were never again fired in wartime. Aircraft with deadly bomb loads replaced these U.S. railway guns. No American railway gun was put out of action during the First World War.

Kaiser Bill's Own Railway War, 1914–18

A mere 10 days before the war's sudden end—on 1 November 1918— the Kaiser was standing with some soldiers outside the parked Imperial train when he glanced skyward in time to see an Allied bomber bearing down on both him and it. His Majesty and his men kept calm—as all the civilians ran for cover—with three whistling aerial bombs exploding close by without any casualties, they containing only enemy propaganda leaflets. All laughed as a frightened cook got up from the ground, with Wilhelm II bawling out, "Idiots!" at the scared civilians. It was only then that the German Supreme Warlord deemed it prudent to arm his own mobile field headquarters train with a complement of machine guns, and this after four years of war. This was accomplished at Imperial General Headquarters' last wartime site, near the oddly named *Hotel Britannique* at Spa, Belgium. For His Majesty, the Great War began as a series of German railroad moves into France, Belgium, and Poland in 1914. For the rest of his time as German Emperor, Wilhelm II's Imperial train would be his mobile field headquarters. On it, he would hurtle to far-flung battlefields, or dart off to Imperial General Headquarters to make him feel wanted, which he was not. Just as during his pre-war railway trips, so now, too, those in wartime were complex, well prepared, and time consuming at all levels. As with his cousin and rival Sovereign the Tsar, all lines over which the Kaiser's train would pass had to be inspected, and then guarded on its way to the fronts. In towns through which it passed, in many cases their residents had to be evacuated for the length of his trip.

The coaches were converted into living rooms, the interior corridors lit with subdued lighting due to possible hostile aircraft overhead. Stops *en route* allowed for dispatch riders to bring His Majesty details of the latest news in the areas in which he was either traveling or due to arrive at. The Kaiser's mobile war room office featured a desk facing a window looking out on to often war-torn areas with bombed out villages passing rapidly by, out of his view. The comfortable, cedar-paneled study had maps of all the various fighting fronts in Europe and the Middle East, so that he could follow the fortunes of his Germanic legions at war. When it halted, cars waiting—flying the Imperial yellow standard—announced his presence thereby. These carried him and the Imperial entourage to spots both allowing the actual front to be seen, as well as being far distant enough, so that His Majesty would not come under enemy fire. So far as is known, he never did, either.

Like any other VIP on either side by these visits, Wilhelm II sought to learn something, as well as to put fresh spirit into the fighting men he saw—and who saw him. Along with an address of under an hour to whatever troops were assembled, His Majesty distributed Iron Cross medals and shook about 300 hands at each such stop. During a field event after the fall of Warsaw to the German Army, one of his generals fainted. Late at night, the Imperial train would then chug back to Kreuznach, or wherever else IGHQ happened to be. On its way, the Kaiser would also see field hospitals, POW trains full of his surrendered enemies, and all manner of destroyed towns and villages, plus incoming troop convoys to reinforce the fighting fronts anew. Even during the war, his critics both within and without Headquarters faulted him for not doing more, the image of both his father and grandfather on horseback in the earlier wars still vivid in their minds. But even they were never subjected to falling aerial bombs and wafting clouds of poison gases.

As Imperial General Headquarters moved from Koblenz to Luxembourg, on to Charleville, away eastwards to Posen and Castle Pless, then back again to Kreuznach, and ultimately to Spa in Belgium—while only briefly at intervals to Berlin—His Majesty's cream and gold train followed in their wake. Reported Imperial memoirist von Kürenburg, "At times, he lived in the Royal train, which assumed a service livery of green…" Ignored by his marshals, generals, admirals, and Reich Chancellor, Wilhelm II moaned in dismay:

The only one who is a bit kind to me is the chief of the Railway Department, who tells me all he does and intends to do.

That this was so—and that the chief turned out to be Gen. Wilhelm Groener—for the Kaiser was one of his eventful life's supreme ironies. Meanwhile, his staff lived on the train as well when His Majesty did, even though it was often cramped; parked on a siding with its twin locomotives.

The Kaiser's Railway-Driven Abdication, 10–11 November 1918

In November 1918, when it was apparent to all in the German High Command that their war was lost, it fell to the then former railways chief— the Bavarian Gen. Groener—to tell the Kaiser that revolt had broken out in the Army and Navy, and also in several large German cities, including the capital of both Prussia and the Reich, Berlin. Other generals present argued the case for sending the Army from the fighting front to fight the revolutionaries at home—the very civil war that His Majesty abhorred. "I shall remain at Spa until an armistice has been signed, and then lead my troops back to Germany," avowed Wilhelm II. Now it was really time for Groener to bite the bullet, and he bluntly told his Kaiser:

> Sire, you no longer have an army! The Army will march home in peace and order under its leaders and commanding generals, but not under the command of Your Majesty—for it no longer stands behind Your Majesty!

At length, the both shocked and enraged Kaiser agreed to abdicate as Emperor—but not as King of Prussia—when in Berlin it was announced instead by the hated Social Democratic leader Philip Scheidemann that he had abdicated from both. Field Marshal von Hindenburg and Gen. Groener then advised him to board the Imperial train and flee to nearby neutral Holland into exile. Both feared the Kaiser's arrest—and even murder—similar to the late Tsar Nicholas II but three months before in Russia—if His Majesty was captured by Red troops in revolt. No one wanted a similar fate to befall the Kaiser and his relatives, least of all Wilhelm II himself. The trip to Holland had to be made that morning of 10 November 1918, if it was to be made at all in safety. What really happened?

One account has him leaving Spa by car driving towards Eysden on the Dutch border, it being stopped by a frontier guard asking for passports.

Left and Below:
The Hotel Britannique
at Spa, the headquarters
where Kaiser Wilhelm II
decided to abdicate on 10
November 1918.

Astonished, the Dutch sentry was told that he was addressing in person the German emperor, asking for admittance into neutral Holland, who handed over his sword to this solitary soldier. Meanwhile, the Imperial train with his newly installed copper bathtub had followed the car to Eysden, where he re-boarded it for an overnight stay, as a site at Dutch Amerongen was being made ready to receive him. Saxe-blue and gold, with black Prussian eagles, it was stocked with both champagne and food to allow his continued living in high style aboard it, just as he always had for the better part of his 30-year-plus reign. Thus fortified, His Majesty spent his last night aboard. On the afternoon of the 11th—after the actual armistice with the Allies had already taken effect behind him—Dutch Count Goddard Bentinck and the governor of the Dutch Province of Utrecht stood waiting in the rain for the train's arrival at Maarn Station near Amerongen. Alighting, Wilhelm II met his two waiting hosts, entering a car for the next leg of this incredible journey into an unexpected and sudden exile.

According to another account 10 cars left Spa in Belgium in a final motorcade, with none of the Imperial standards affixed, at 5 a.m. on 10 November 1918. His Majesty, however, was neither on the train nor in this 10-car convoy, but instead was in an 11th, separate car with an entourage of three, detouring in an arc to rendezvous with the "official" convoy some distance away from Spa. The 10 cars were a ruse for his protection from Red troops possibly sent to waylay him, as had been Nicholas II in Russia on his Imperial train. The Kaiser reached Eysden at 7 a.m., and waited in the nearby station for his summoned train to join him. His Majesty had traveled already for the last time in the train that had taken him to so many European capitals, and across blackened First World War battlefields that were all part of history now. Later that day, Count Bentinck's car crossed the bridge over his moated castle at Amerongen, with gates guarded by Dutch Army—and not German—sentries. Feeling safe for the first moment since he had motored away from Spa, Wilhelm II gleefully rubbed his hands together and chortled to his started host the count, "And now for a cup of real, good English tea!" an incongruous end to his more than 4½-year war against the British Empire that he had just lost.

In yet another account, the Kaiser had been forced to cool his heels for six hours in the sparse railway station—a novel experience for him!—as the neutral Dutch government of Queen Wilhelmina debated what to do with their unexpected Royal visitor: to grant him the desired political asylum or not? As this continued, the Imperial train arrived, and the Kaiser's party re-boarded it to spend the night. On 28 November 1918, his Kaiserin Dona arrived as well safely in Holland, after having herself faced

Red Guard soldiers in the Berlin Palace on her own. On that same 28 November 1918, Wilhelm II signed the Formal Act of Abdication papers releasing all soldiers and other servants of the Crown from their oaths of allegiance to him. Crown Prince Wilhelm had arrived in Holland as well on 12 November 1918, but did not see his father, being sent off instead to his own exile on a Dutch island in the Zuyder Zee. He, too, abdicated all rights of succession to His Majesty. But exactly how had the Kaiser reached the Dutch frontier, really? The final account demands a precise rendering, thus: the journey's confusion was most likely designed to keep secret His Majesty's exact movements. Scheduled for 5 a.m., the train actually slid away at 4:30, the direct route to the Dutch border being but 20 miles, with the railway trip being decidedly roundabout. At 2 a.m., the Kaiser's driver in Spa was told to prepare the Royal motor—without insignia—for a lengthy trip; 10 cars left Spa simultaneously as did the train, but then met another vehicle coming in the opposite direction, with Wilhelm II and the trio of officers. Near 7 a.m., the column arrived at the Eysden Village. Alighting, the men walked a short distance to the station, with the cars following behind. Shortly after, the Royal train trundled in, to serve as the Kaiser's residence. His Majesty encountered his host Count Bentinck on the afternoon of Armistice Day, 11 November 1918, at the little railway station at Maarn, close by the small town of Rhenen, and closed to the public.

The Kaiser waits to enter Holland.
Bundesarchiv

Only Dutch Province of Utrecht Governor Count Lynden was present at the Kaiser's arrival, as a gaggle of railway men and curious villagers leaned on the wooden gates of the station. There was both thick fog and a driving rain, giving the quiet scene an air of depression. On another train—traveling from Istanbul home to Germany via the Ukraine—a future leader of the now defeated German Army, Col. Gen. Hans von Seeckt—received the news of His Majesty's departure from Holland by rail. With tears in his eyes, von Seeckt reflected that the army had lost its "Royal Shield," as he himself had once termed the final German emperor—thus far.

German Imperial Crown Prince Wilhelm's Train War, 1914–18

In his 1922 memoirs, the former German Imperial Crown Prince Wilhelm recalled operational weak spots of their right wing in Belgium and the left at Verdun in France thus:

> Our railways would not permit us to evacuate rapidly the extensive war zone beyond the Antwerp–Meuse position, so that immense quantities of munitions and stores would fall into the hands of the enemy.... The Antwerp–Meuse line would form an unfavorable permanent position, since the railways—having no lateral communications—would render the transport of troops behind the front and from one wing to another cumbrous and slow.... The loss of material and the unfavorable railway facilities could not be helped.... In the larger camps on the lines of communication, thousands of straggling shirkers and men on leave wandered about.... Some of them were totally unable to join their regiments on account of the overburdening of the railways.

The German Crown Prince as an army group commander called it right in the fall of 1914 with the introduction of stalemate trench warfare when he predicted that, "The war is lost. It will go on for a long time, but lost it is already." Late in 1918, the signs of revolution were also visible to the Kaiser's Heir to the Throne:

> A few kilometers from Waulsort—just as we reached a spot where the railway runs close beside the high road—we saw a leave train which had halted and was flying the Red flag. Immediately afterwards—from the open or broken windows—my ears were greeted with the stupid cries of, "Lights out, knives out!" which formed a sort of catchword and cry for all the hooligans and malcontents of that period. I stopped my car

and—accompanied by Zobeltitz—walked up to the train. I ordered the men to alight, which they did at once. There may have been 500–600 of them…. The men began to press towards us, and I addressed them in urgent tones, endeavoring to touch their sense of honor. Even while I was speaking, I could see that I had won the contest.

The date was 7 November 1918, three days before the Kaiser's own departure for Holland. "I made my first personal acquaintance with the revolution."

During his own subsequent flight to exile in Holland, the Crown Prince passed briefly through the railway junction of Laroche:

It is a terrible chaos through which we drive: bawling … shouts and screams; and the storming of the trains…. We pass under a narrow railway arch…. The yelling and bawling at the railway station reverberates over our heads.

On 23 November 1918, safely in Holland, Wilhelm recalled, "The train leaves Roermond station at seven o'clock. A Dutch captain is appointed as our companion."

The First Railway Dining Car Armistice at Compiègne, France, November 1918

At Tergnier, France on Friday, 8 November 1918, the German Armistice Commission arrived by automobile at a small railway junction at 3 a.m., French time. Waiting for the members was a French chasseur cavalry company at the railway station's ruins. As the German armistice delegation departed its cars, the French horsemen presented arms in salute, the downcast representatives treading gingerly to a railroad car standing silent. Climbing aboard were Major General Detlev von Winterfeldt and Count Aldred von Oberndorff. Detlev von Winterfeldt saw a huge delayed action explosive hole next to the track. Explained Frenchman Bourbon-Busset:

It exploded three weeks after the German Army left. I hope there are not any others under our train. I would not want to see you blown up—or me, either.

Aboard, he and the German delegation found they were on the 1860 personal saloon car of the late deposed Emperor of the French, Napoleon

III, featuring interior green satin upholstery emblazoned still with the famed Napoleonic bee iconography. It depicted as well the monogrammed *N*. In 1870, the defeated Emperor of the French was forced at Sedan to surrender in humiliating fashion to Bismarck. Now that it was the Germans' turn to surrender, the French had brought his coach out of retirement to add to their despair. One eyewitness noted:

> The windows were shut and the curtains drawn so that the Germans could not see out. They asked where they were going, but the French still would not say.... The delegates were offered brandy as the train pulled out of the station. Then they settled down to sleep in their clothes, getting what rest they could before arriving at their final destination, wherever that might be.

As they bore on through the darkness Field Marshal Ferdinand Foch and the Allied Armistice Commission awaited their arrival north of Paris in a dark, gloomy, and isolated clearing in the Compiègne Forest. This was not far from where the Paris Gun had shelled the French capital less than two months previously, but now the site was surrounded by French Army sentries on guard.

This concealed cutting in the woods near Rethondes railway station had previously served as a French artillery battery location from which to bombard the battered German Army, and now it would witness its historic submission as well, hidden away from all journalists. Arriving by rail from Marshal Foch's Senlis headquarters the night before, the Armistice Commission train comprised two sleeping cars, a pair of second class passenger coaches, and Foch's soon-to-be-world-famous dining car with a large table across which the negotiations would transpire. Having slept that night aboard, at 7 a.m. on the day that the negotiations started, Foch and the others were waiting, as the German train halted 100 yards away. The Germans were still unaware of their location. The French remained silent on that point until the arrival of French Army Gen. Maxime Weygand, Foch's chief of staff, who informed the Germans that Marshal Foch would receive them in two hours in the train opposite theirs. One report of the event noted:

> They walked across on the wooden duckboards connecting the two railway spurs... The delegates were shown to the dining car by Gen. Weygand. The car had telephones, a map of the front line, and a large conference table with four place cards on either side. Weygand motioned them to the German side and went to fetch Foch, who was waiting for them in the next carriage.... The atmosphere was stiff and tense as Foch

entered.... He asked to see the delegation's credentials. The documents were handed over, and Foch took them back to the other carriage to examine them with British Royal Navy Vice-Admiral Sir Rosslyn Wemyss.

Back in the dining car, Foch asked the Germans why they had come. "What do you want of me?" he demanded. At length, the Germans formally asked him for an armistice. Gen. Weygand read the Allied armistice terms, among them that, "5,000 locomotives and 150,000 railways cars in good condition" would be delivered by Germany to France in 14 days. Returning to their own train, the Germans conferred hurriedly.... At 11:30 a.m., Gen. Winterfeldt returned across the duckboards to send a radio message to Spa. The deadline for the armistice to be signed and go into effect was 11 November 1918.

Meanwhile, the Munich Railway Station in Bavaria was occupied by German Red revolutionaries on the 8th. In Berlin, "Train services had been suspended to prevent an influx of troublemakers" that same day as well. Just after 2 a.m. on the 11th, Adm. Wemyss was called: the German delegation was ready to talk, and was coming back to the dining car again, to make peace. All the delegates filed into the dining car, carriage 2419D of the Wagon-Lits Company. The absent Marshal von Hindenburg worried that the German economy would collapse if they were forced to hand over all the carriages demanded by his opposite number, Marshal Foch, so renewed haggling went on until just after 5 a.m., when the crestfallen Germans signed the armistice terms.

Marshal Foch himself left the ultimate eyewitness account as one of the actual participants in his postwar 1931 memoirs:

It was ... a spot in the Compiègne Forest north of and near the Rethondes station. My train was there, run onto a siding built for railroad artillery.... The German delegation [had been] ... halted by the blocked condition of the roads behind the German front, and reached the French lines only at 9 p.m., and arrived at their destination 12 hours late. It was not until 7 a.m. on 8 November 1918 that the train bringing them drew up near mine; two hours later—at 9 a.m.—the first meeting took place in the office car of the French train....

After the signing on the 11th, Foch made his official Report to the French premier and President of the French Republic Raymond Poincaré, who on 23 August 1918, had personally handed Foch his baton as a newly named Marshal of France. The official report of the event noted:

The Marshal's train—and the one on which the German plenipotentiaries had taken at Tergniers—were lying on sidings built for railway artillery in the Foret de l'Aigle, near the Rethondes station.... The French Marshal was adamant: "Hostilities cannot cease before the signing of the armistice!" The Germans protested, "The German Army is beset by unimaginable difficulties," including, "blocking of roads and railways that paralyzes all movement.... Moreover, Germany is threatened with famine. The armistice clauses touching [the Royal Naval] blockade and railway material are inhumane, because they will paralyze the work of feeding the population, and will cause the death of women and children." Still, Foch would not budge.

From Berlin, the last Imperial Chancellor Prince Max von Baden accepted the Allied terms during 8–9 p.m., as did Field Marshal von Hindenburg for the German General Staff at 9 p.m. Among the official Conditions agreed upon was # 7: "Roads and means of communications of every kind—railways, roads, waterways, bridges, telegraph, telephones—shall be in no manner impaired. All civil and military personnel ... employed on them shall remain; 5,000 locomotives and 150,000 freight cars in good working order—with all necessary spare parts and fittings—shall be delivered to the Associated Parties within the period fixed ... not exceeding 31 days in all; 5,000 motor trucks are also to be delivered in good order within 36 days. The railways of Alsace-Lorraine shall be handed over within 31 days, together with all personnel and material belonging to the organization of the system.... All stores of coal and material for the upkeep of permanent way, signals, and repair shops shall be kept ... in an efficient state by Germany ... as the means of communication on the left bank of the Rhine...

Gen. Weygand said of the German delegation members: "Their train left the Rethondes station at 11:30 a.m. for Tergnier, where they were to take their automobiles" back to their own lines.

Marshal Foch concluded:

On 11 November 1918, at 11 a.m., firing ceased along the whole front of the Allied armies. An impressive silence followed upon 53 weeks of battle.... The next day, I issued the following General Order: "You have won the greatest battle in history!... You have full right to be proud, for you have crowned your standards with immortal glory" of the Allied armies. The war thus ceased in place.

Above: Members of the German Armistice Commission (left) enter Marshal Foch's dining car at Compiègne, from left to right: German Army Maj. Gen. Detlev von Winterfeldt, former military attaché in Paris; Naval Capt. Ernst Vanselow (saluting, hand to cap visor); French officer; delegation chief Reichstag Catholic Centrist Party leader Matthias Erzberger (in civilian bowler hat); and another French officer. *Library of Congress*

Left: A popular postcard of the signing of the armistice, 11 November 1918.

415. - Photographie prise le 11 Novembre 1918 à 7 h. 30, au moment où le Maréchal Foch part pour Paris remettre au gouvernement français le texte de l'Armistice qui vient d'être signé avec l'Allemagne.

1. Maréchal Foch
2. Amiral Sir R. Wemyss
3. Général Weygand
4. Contre-Amiral G. Hope
5. Captain Marriott

6. Général Desticker
7. Capitaine de Mierry
8. Commandant Riedinger
9. Officier-Interprète Laperche

Cliché Pupier
Reproduction interdite

Defeated Germany & Austria, 1918

After his abrupt dismissal by the Kaiser, the fall of all the German dynasties, and the ascent of the Reich's own Red revolution, Gen. Ludendorff fled the fallen Second Reich in fear for his life, in disguise. Left behind and terrified, his first wife Margarethe later left Berlin to rejoin her husband, in an exodus described as both difficult and even hazardous. A Capt. Fischer was her protective escort, and helped get them onto a train leaving from Berlin's Stettin Station on 22 December 1918.

Margarethe Ludendorff recalled the event later:

> The carriages were packed with soldiers, and crammed with knapsacks, trunks, and suitcases. Dust and dirt reigned everywhere. The soldiers wore visible traces of their long marches and railway journeys, perspiring and unwashed, in many cases caked with mud, as they had left the trenches.... They were the last rearguard from the front.

No regular seating being at hand, they found at least some floor space in a car's corridor, with Margarethe Ludendorff sitting on Capt. Fischer's knees, with he atop her luggage. She was verbally subjected to hearing her husband and the Kaiser cursed at by a huge soldier squatting near them, all in a smell that made her almost faint. Thus did her trip continue for almost a full day and night in the cold, as they both feared discovery. Worse was to come at the frontier, where guards stripped her down to her chemise, and searched, "All down my body to the soles of my feet!" As with her general husband before her, so, too, did Mrs. Ludendorff safely escape the now partially Red Reich.

Von Bülow's Postwar Memoirs on Trains

Former German Imperial Chancellor Bernhard von Bülow (1900–09) published his four-volume memoirs posthumously during 1930–32, blasting his former boss, Kaiser Wilhelm II. The volume covering 1909–19 is very interesting in that he maintained contact with his previous colleagues while out of office, and also was in the Reich capital of Berlin during the whole of the Red revolution that helped overthrow the Hohenzollern dynasty. In Vol. 3—*The World War and Germany's Collapse, 1909–1918*—he noted of his farewell train ride into exile—aping that of Bismarck in 1890—from Berlin on 17 July 1909:

Jubilation in Swansea, South Wales. There was jubilation throughout the countries making up the Western Alliance.

German prisoners of war in France.

Demobilized German soldiers entrained on their way home to the Reich.

I … sat opposite my wife in the saloon car, transformed by the kindness of many friends into a bower of roses, carnations, and orchids in her honor…. The train bore us from Berlin to Hamburg … We passed through Spandau, the ancient residence of the first Hohenzollern electors…. The train pulled up at Ludwigslust, which I had often visited as a boy…. The towers of Hamburg came into view…. At the station [Albert] Ballin and Felix von Eckhardt were awaiting us; a great crowd had gathered to give us welcome. Had I been recalled [to office] before the end of July 1914, I could have prevented the outbreak of war…. Had I been consulted before the ultimatum was handed to Serbia, I should have advised against this piece of folly with all the urgent strength I might have used to arouse a signalman I had found asleep at his post at the moment when two expresses were due to cross….

Recalling that summer of 1914, von Bülow remembered:

In five days, Germany had mobilized—everything went through without a hitch…. [again, another tribute to the hapless Helmuth von Moltke the Younger] Then came the transport of troops to east and west, with not one single unforeseen delay! Never once did the necessity arise of applying for further instructions to the General Staff in Berlin…. When—

on 3 August 1914—there followed our declaration of war on France....
It was easy enough for the French to prove conclusively that no French
airman had dropped bombs on the railway from Nurnberg to Ingolstadt.

Postwar, von Moltke wrote to Bülow concerning the successful
mobilization of summer 1914:

> The credit for that must go to the whole staff ... who worked so well to
> bring this Army—a million strong—into position, but especially to the
> staff of the transport section.

During his way to and from train stations during his retirement years, von
Bülow recalled, people bowed to him and his wife in transit. Of his return
from Rome in 1915, he remembered:

> On my journey back into Germany, the Swiss authorities welcomed
> me most courteously at the frontier. At Karlsruhe, I was met by a
> representative of the Grand Duchess Louise, who tendered me that
> sovereign's thanks for my patriotic efforts in Rome. Jagow—in Berlin—
> had spread a report that I should not be returning immediately. He
> hoped by this to prevent any reception, at the Anhalter Bahnhof, in
> my honor, although I myself had not wanted one. Next day—in every
> paper it could command—the Foreign Office published sarcastic little
> paragraphs to the effect that—at the station—the only people there
> to receive me had been a hall porter and the proprietor of the Hotel
> Adlon.... I had read with real grief—at the Flottbek station—the names
> of the sons of Flottbek who had already laid down their lives for King
> and Country, Empire and Emperor.

Regarding the 1918 revolution, von Bülow recalled:

> On 5 November 1918, the Soviet Ambassador—Adolf Joffe—was at
> last expelled from Berlin for his propaganda. Some defective postbags—
> addressed to his embassy—had burst open on the station platform,
> discharging a shower of revolutionary pamphlets in German, and so had
> furnished irrefutable proof that Joffe considered it his mission to foment
> revolution in Germany ...

Perhaps just as Wilhelm II had done in Russia in April 1917. The train
wheel, indeed, had come full circle.

Bibliography

General Reference Works

Grolier Encyclopedia, Vol. 5 & 8, edited by S. Edgar Farquhar, MS, New York, The Grolier Society Publishers, 1946

General Train Reference Works

A *Guide to Trains: The World's Greatest Trains, Tracks, and Travel* by Consultant Editor David Jackson, San Francisco, Fog City Express, 2002

B & O Railroad Museum: The Birthplace of American Railroading, Baltimore, MD 21223

Blood, Iron & Gold: How the Railroads Transformed the World by Christian Wolmar, New York, Public Affairs, 2010

Die Anderen Nurnberger Technische Speilzeug aus der "Guten Alten Zeit/" Band 2 by J. Falk, Frankfurt-am-Main, Hobby Haas, 1973

Die Einheits-Personen-und Gepackwagen der Deutschen Reichsbahn: Bauarten Regelspur, 1932–37 by Joachim Deppmeyer, Stuttgart, Abend, 1988

Dorpmullers Reichsbahn: Die Ara des Reichsverkehrsministers Julius Dorpmuller, 1920–45 by Dr Alfred Gottwaldt, Freiburg, Eisenbahn Kurier-Verlag, 2009

Der Rote Teppich: Geschichte de Staatszuge und Salonwagen by Paul Dost, Stuttgart, Franckh'sche Verlagshandlung, 1965

German versus British Railways with Special Reference to Owner's Risk and Trader's Claims by Edwin A. Pratt, London, P. S. King & Sons, 1907

Illustrated Book of Steam and Rail: The History and Development of the Train and an Evocative Guide to the World's Great Railway Journeys by

Colin Garratt and Max Wade-Matthews, New York, Barnes & Noble, 2003

The Encylopedia of Trains and Locomotives by C. J. Riley, New York, Michael Friedman Publishing Group, Inc., 2002

The Encyclopedia of Trains and Locomotives: The Comprehensive Guide to Over 900 Steam, Diesel, and Electric Locomotives from 1825 to the Present Day by General Editor David Ross, San Diego, Thunder Bay Press, 2003

Engines of War: How Wars Were Won & Lost on the Railways by Christian Wolmar, New York, Public Affairs Books, 2010

The Great Book of Trains by Brian Hollingsworth and Arthur Cook, London, Salamander Books, 2003

The Rise of Rail-Power in War and Conquest, 1833–1914 by Edwin A. Pratt, London, P. S. King & Son, Ltd., 1915

Trains by John Coiley, London, Dorling Kindersley, 2000

Supplying War: Logistics from Wallenstein to Patton by Martin Van Crefeld, London, Cambridge University Press, 1977

Fifty Railroads that Changed the Course of History by Bill Laws, Richmond Hill, Ontario, Firefly Books, 2013

The Bismarckian Era, 1862–90

The Age of Empires edited by Robert Aldrich, New York, Thames & Hudson, 2007

The Army of the German Empire, 1870–88 by Albert Seaton & Michael Youens, London, Osprey Publishing, Ltd., 1973

Bismarck by Werner Richter, London, Macdonald, 1964

Bismarck: The Man and the Statesman by A. J. P. Taylor, New York, Alfred A. Knopf, 1955

1848: Year of Revolution by Mike Rapport, New York, Basic Books, 2008

An Uncommon Woman: The Empress Frederick—Daughter of Queen Victoria, Wife of the Crown Prince of Prussia, Mother of Kaiser Wilhelm by Hannah Pakula, New York, Simon & Schuster, 1995

Brady's Civil War Journal: Photographing the War, 1861–65 by Theodore P. Savas, New York, Skyhorse Publishing, 2008

Dearest Vicky, Darling Fritz: Queen Victoria's Eldest Daughter and the German Emperor by John van der Kiste, Stroud, Sutton Publishing Ltd., 2001

Diaries of the Emperor Frederick During the Campaigns of 1866 and 1870–71, as Well as His Journeys to the East and to Spain edited by Margarethe von Poschinger, London, Chapman & Hall, Ltd., 1902

The Franco-Prussian War by Michael Howard, Dorset Press, 1961

The Franco-Prussian War: The German Conquest of France in 1870–71 by Geoffrey Wawro, New York, Cambridge University Press, 2003

Frederick III: Germany's Liberal Emperor by Patricia Kollander, Westport, CT, Greenwood Press, 1995

Frederick III: German Emperor, 1888 by John Van der Kiste, Gloucester, Alan Sutton, 1981

The French Millenium: 1,000 Remarkable Years of Incident and Achievement by Nick Yapp, Koln, Konemann, 2001

The German Millennium: 1,000 Remarkable Years of Incident and Achievement by Nick Yapp, Koln, Konemann, 2000

German Military Forces of the 19th Century by Gustav A. Sigel & Maj. Gen. von Specht, New York, Military Press, 1989

Gold and Iron: Bismarck, Bleichröder and the Building of the German Empire by Fritz Stern, New York, Vintage Books, 1979

The Great Train Race: Railways and the Franco-German Rivalry, 1815–1914 by Allan Mitchell, New York, Berghahn Books, 2000

History of the German Army by Keith Simpson, New York, Military Press, 1985

History of the German General Staff, 1657–1945 by Walter Gorlitz, New York, Praeger Paperbacks, 1962

The New Illustrated History of the World: Industrial Revolution, 1848–1917 by David Gillard, New York, Paul Hamlyn, 1970

Solferino 1859: The Battle for Italy's Freedom by Richard Brooks and Peter Dennis, New York, Osprey Publishing Ltd., 2009

Napoleon III and His Carnival Empire by John Bierman, New York, St. Martin's Press, 1988

Prussian Memories 1864–1914 by Poultney Bigelow, New York: G. P. Putnam's Sons, 1915

The Year of the Three Kaisers: Bismarck and the German Succession, 1887–88 by J. Alden Nichols, Urbana, IL, University of Illinois Press, 1987

Tsarist Russian Railways

A Picture History of Russia edited by John Stuart Martin, New York, Crown Publishers, Inc., 1968

The Bolsheviks and the Czechoslovak Legion by Victor M. Fic, New Delhi: Abhinav, 1978

The Court of the Last Tsar: Pomp, Power, and Pageantry in the Reign of Nicholas II by Greg King, Hoboken, NJ, John Wiley & Sons, Inc., 2006

The Czech Legion, 1914–20 by David Bullock and Ramiro Bujeiro, Oxford, Oxford University Press, 2007

The Czech & Slovak Legion in Siberia, 1917–22 by Joan McGuire Mohr, NC: McFarland, 2012

The Czechoslovak Legion in Russia, 1914–20 by John Bradley, Boulder, CO: East European Monographs, 1990

The Escape of Alexei: Son of Tsar Nicholas—What Happened When the Romanov Family was Executed by Vadim Petrov, Igor Lysenko, & Georgi Egorov, New York: Harry N. Abrams, Inc., Publishers, 1998

The File on the Tsar by Anthony Summers & Tom Mangold, New York: Jove/HBJ, 1976

The Life and Death of Lenin by Robert Payne, New York, Simon & Schuster, 1964

The Lost Fortune of the Tsars by William Clarke, New York: St. Martin's Press, 1994

The March of the 70,000 by Henry Baerlein, London: Leonard Parsons/ Whitefriar Press, 1926

Nicholas and Alexandra: An Intimate Account of the Last of the Romanovs and the Fall of Imperial Russia by Robert K. Massie, New York, Athenaeum, New York, 1967

Nicholas and Alexandra: The Last Imperial Family of Tsarist Russia, State Hermitage Museum and the State Archive of the Russian Federation, London, Booth-Cliburn Editions, 1998

Road to Power: The Trans-Siberian Railroad and the Colonization of Asian Russia, 1850–1917 by S. G. Marks, 1991

The Romanovs: The Final Chapter by Robert K. Massie, New York: Random House, 1995

The Romanovs, 1613–1918 by Simon Sebag Montefiore, New York: Alfred A. Knopf Publishing, 2016

The Sealed Train: Lenin's Eight-Month Journey from Exile to Power by Michael Pearson, New York, G. P. Putnam's Sons, 1975

The Siberian Intervention by John Albert White, Princeton, NJ: Princeton University Press, 1950

To the Great Ocean: Siberia and the Trans-Siberian Railway by Harmon Tupper, New York: Little, Brown, 1965

To the Edge of the World by Christian Wolmar, New York: Public Affairs, 2013

Tsar: The Lost World of Nicholas and Alexandra by Peter Kurth, Boston; Little, Brown, and Company, 1998

The Wilhelmine Kaiserreich Era, 1888–1918

Berlin–Baghdad Railway by F. William Engdahl, 1993

The Berlin–Baghdad Express: The Ottoman Empire & Germany's Bid for World Power by Sean McMeekin, Cambridge, MA: Harvard University Press, 2010

The Berlin–Baghdad Railway as a Cause of World War I by Arthur P. Malloney, Alexandria, VA, Center for Naval Analyses, 1984

Bully Boy: The Truth About Theodore Roosevelt's Legacy by Jim Powell, New York, Crown Forum, 2006

The Construction of the Baghdad Railway and Its Impact on Anglo-Turkish Relations, 1902–13 by Mustafa Sitki, BILGIN

Der Hofzug: Sr. Majestat des Deutschen Kaisers, Konigs von Preussen, by Dr Alfred Gottwaldt

The Diplomatic History of the Baghdad Railroad by John B. Wolf, Columbia, MO: The University of Missouri, 1936

Distant Ties: Germany, the Ottoman Empire, and the Construction of the Baghdad Railway by Jonathan S. McMurray, Westport, CT: Prager Publishing, 2001

Eclipse of Kings: European Monarchies in the 20th Century by Denis Judd, New York, Stein & Day, 1976

The Entourage of Kaiser Wilhelm II, 1888–1918 by Isabel V. Hull, New York, Cambridge University Press, 1982

The Ex-Kaiser in Exile by Lady Norah Bentinck, New York, George H. Doran Co.

The Fall of the Kaiser by Maurice Baumont, New York, Alfred A. Knopf, 1931

George, Nicholas, and Wilhelm: Three Royal Cousins and the Road to World War I by Miranda Carter, New York, Alfred A. Knopf, 2010

The Great Naval Game: Britain and Germany in the Age of Empire by Jan Ruger, New York, Cambridge University Press, 2007

Kaiser Wilhelm II: New Interpretations edited by John C. G. Rohl and Nicolaus Sombart, New York, Cambridge University Press, 2005

Kaiser and Fuhrer: A Comparative Study of Personality and Politics by Robert G. L. Waite, Toronto, University Press, 1998

The Kaiser: A Life of Wilhelm II, Last Emperor of Germany by Joachim von Kürenberg, New York, Simon and Schuster, 1955

The Kaiser and His Court: Wilhelm II and the Government of Germany by John C. G. Rohl, New York, Cambridge University Press, 1987

The Kaiser's Army in Color: Uniforms of the Imperial German Army as Illustrated by Carl Becker, 1890–1910 by Charles Wooley, Atglen, PA, Schiffer Military History Books, 2000

The Kaiser's Memoirs by Kaiser Wilhelm II, Emperor of Germany, 1888–1918; New York, Harper & Brothers Publishers, 1922

The Kaiser and His Times by Michael Balfour, Boston, Houghton-Mifflin Co., 1964

The Kaiser: New Research in Wilhelm II's Role in Imperial Germany edited by Annika Mombauer and Wilhelm Deist, New York, Cambridge University Press, 2003

The Kaiser's Daughter: Memoirs of HRH Viktoria Luise, Princess of Prussia, Englewood, NJ, Prentice-Hall, Inc., 1977

King, Kaiser, Tsar: Three Royal Cousins Who Led the World to War by Catrine Clay, New York, Walker & Co., 2006

Knaves, Fools, and Heroes in Europe Between the Wars by Sir John Wheeler-Bennett, New York, St. Martin's Press, 1974

The Last Kaiser: A Biography of Wilhelm II, German Emperor and King of Prussia by Tyler Whittle, New York, Times Books, 1977

The Last Kaiser: The Life of Wilhelm II by Giles Macdonough, New York, St. Martin's Press, 2000

The Memoirs of the Crown Prince of Germany, London, Thornton Butterworth, Ltd., 1922

The Memoirs of Prince von Bülow: Secretary of State to Imperial Chancellor, 1897–1903, Vol. 1, Boston; Little, Brown, and Co., 1931

The Memoirs of Prince von Bülow: From the Morocco Crisis to Resignation, 1903–09, Vol. 2, Boston; Little, Brown, and Co., 1931

The Memoirs of Prince von Bülow: The World War and Germany's Collapse, 1909–19, Vol. 3, Boston; Little, Brown, and Co., 1932

The Memoirs of Prince von Bülow: Early Years and Diplomatic Service, 1849–97, Vol. 4, Boston; Little, Brown, and Co., 1932

The Mysterious Last "Train Ride" of Wilhelm II—His Imperial "Reise Kaiser" by Blaine Taylor, Towson, MD (previously unpublished manuscript)

My Early Life by William II, Ex-Emperor of Germany, New York, George H. Doran Co., 1926

Railways and International Politics: Paths of Empire, 1848–1945 edited by T. G. Otte and Keith Neilson, New York, Routledge, 2009

Reischbahn-Salonwagen/National Railway Salon Car by Walter Haberling, 2009

The Train That Disappeared Into History: The Berlin-to-Baghdad Railway and How It Lead to the Great War by Kathie Somerset-Ayrton, Soesterberg, The Netherlands: Uitgeverij Aspekt, 2007

Wilhelm II: Emperor and Exile, 1900–1941, Vol. 2 by Lamar Cecil, Chapel Hill, The University of North Carolina Press, 1996

Wilhelm II: The Kaiser's Personal Monarchy, 1888–1900, Vol. 2 by John C. G. Rohl, New York, Cambridge University Press, 2004

Young Wilhelm: The Kaiser's Early Life, 1859–88, Vol. 1 by John C. G. Rohl, New York, Cambridge University Press, 1998

The Great War, 1914–18

1918: The Last Act by Barrie Pitt, New York, Ballantine Books, 1963

Brest-Litovsk: The Forgotten Peace, March 1918 by Sir John Wheeler-Bennett, New York: W. W. Norton & Co., 1960

Dreams of a Great Small Nation: The Mutinous Army that Threatened a Revolution, Destroyed an Empire, Founded a Republic, and Remade the Map of Europe by Kevin J. McNamara, New York: Public Affairs, 2016

Duel for Kilimanjaro: Africa, 1914–18/The Dramatic Story of an Unconventional War by Leonard Mosley, New York, Ballantine Books, 1963

The First World War: A Photographic History edited by Laurence Stallings, New York, Simon & Schuster, 1933

The German High Command at War: Hindenburg and Ludendorff Conduct World War I by Robert B. Asprey, New York, William A. Morrow and Co., Inc., 1991

The Great War by Cyril Falls, New York, G. P. Putnam's Sons, 1959

The Great War by Field Marshal von Hindenburg, St. Paul, MN, MBI Publishing, 2006

The Greatest Day in History: How, on the 11th Hour of the 11th Day of the 11th Month, the First World War Finally Came to an End by Nicholas Best, New York, Public Affairs, 2008

The Guns of August by Barbara Tuchman, New York, Macmillan, 1962

Hedjaz Railway by R. Touret, Touret Publishing, 1989

The Hejaz Railway by James Nicholson, Stacey International Publishers

Helmuth von Moltke and the Origins of the First World War by Annika Mombauer, New York, Cambridge University Press, 2001

Lawrence of Arabia's War: The Arabs, the British, and the Remaking of the Middle East in WWI by Neil Faulkner, New Haven, CT: Yale University Press, 2016

Ludendorff: Genius of World War I by John Goodspeed, Boston, Houghton Mifflin & Co., 1966

The Marne: August 1914—The Heroism and Horror of the Epic Battle That Turned the Tide of World War I by Georges Blond, New York, Pyramid Books, 1966

The Marne: The Opening of World War I and the Battle That Changed the World by Holger H. Herwig, New York, Random House, 2009

The Memoirs of Marshal Foch by Generalissimo Ferdinand Foch, Garden City, NY: Doubleday, Doran & Co., 1931

My Four Years in Germany by James W. Gerard, New York: Grosset & Dunlap Publishers 1917

On to Kilimanjaro by Brian Gardner, New York, Macfadden-Bartell Books, 1964

Opening Moves: August 1914 by John Keegan, New York, Ballentine Books, 1971

Paris 1919: Six Months That Changed the World by Margaret Macmillan, New York, Random House, 2003

Seven Pillars of Wisdom: A Triumph by T. E. Lawrence, New York: Anchor Books, 1991

The Price of Glory: Verdun 1916 by Alistair Horne, New York, Macfadden-Bartell Books, 1964

Tormented Warrior: Ludendorff and the Supreme Command by Roger Parkinson, New York, Stein & Day, 1979

When the Cheering Stopped: The Last Years of Woodrow Wilson by Gene Smith, New York, William Morrow and Co., 1964

Articles

A Century of Russian Railroad Construction: 1837–1936 by Edward Ames, American Slavic & East European Review 6, (3/4), 57-74, 1947

Beijing to Hamburg fast cargo rail link planned, The China Post, 11 Jan. 2008

German Railway Constructions in Germany and the Middle East, 1835–1939 by Pinhas Walter Pick, pp. 72-85

Moltke-Conrad: Relations Between the Austro-Hungarian and German General Staffs, 1909–14 by Norman Stone, Cambridge University Press: The Historical Journal, Vol. 9, #2 (1966), pp. 201–228

"That Bohemian Corporal: Adolf Hitler in World War I by Blaine Taylor, San Diego, The Military Advisor, Summer 2008

The 1905 Revolution on the Siberian Railroad by Henry Reichman, Russian Review 47 (1): 25-48, 1988

The Great Siberian Iron Road, The Daily News, London, 30 December 1896, p. 7.